TWEETS OF LOVE AND PROTEST

ASEMANA BOOKS

TWEETS OF LOVE AND PROTEST

A Poetic Inquiry into Writing of Emotions in Social Movements

Amir Kalan

ASEMANA BOOKS

Toronto, Canada

FIRST EDITION

Copyright © 2026 by Asemana Books

ALL RIGHTS RESERVED.
No part of this book may be reproduced or transmitted in any form or by any means, electronic or mechanical, including photocopying, recording, or by any information storage and retrieval system, without prior written permission from the publisher, except for the inclusion of brief quotations in a review.
Published by ASEMANA BOOKS
ISBN: 978-1-997503-38-5
Book Design: Asemana Books
Cover Art: Asemana Books

To find out more about our authors and books visit: www.asemanabooks.ca

ASEMANA
BOOKS

This book is the outcome of an interdisciplinary humanities project that draws on multiple fields, including sociology, political science, communication studies, cultural studies, and writing studies. Part of my broader *Writing in Times of Crisis* project, this publication offers the findings of a poetic inquiry into the emotional dimensions of political resistance, based on a collection of tweets posted during a series of protests in Iran between December 2017 and May 2022. In order to address the disciplinary diversity and emotional complexity involved in the project, I have employed poetic inquiry as a methodology that could help generate language and themes that best represent the intricacies of the issue at hand.

This book is composed of two parts. The first is a curated selection of short poems that emerged from the collected tweets. The poems were constructed through what I call "refractive poetic analysis," a method that lies between found and generated poetry. The second part of the book is a chapter in prose that offers theoretical and methodological context, reflecting on how poetic inquiry can serve as an interpretive and expressive tool for understanding the affective registers of social resistance. My approach uses poetry not only as representation but also as analysis—blurring the line between the voices of the Twitter users and my own, to foreground the collective emotional terrain of experiences with protest.

Social media platforms such as Twitter, currently named X, generate a carnivalesque space that permits diverse participation and expression. However, while these platforms allow the expression of multiple voices, they can at the same time hide such posts through intentional algorithms that favor certain trends. The book explores this algorithmically isolated space as a valuable archive. It unearths the tweets in this space to show how emotionally charged digital utterances can be reframed poetically to make the inner worlds of protesters and witnesses legible. In doing so, I hope to contribute to arts-based and research-creation inquiry methods that aim to amplify subaltern voices and intervene in dominant political narratives.

THUS TWOTE ZARATHUSTRA: A REFRACTIVE POETIC RECOMPOSITION

THEY

they butcher every word so ruthlessly
that after each sentence they utter
their teeth and chins are covered in blood
poor words!
poor truth!

do they spoil you?
does everyone love you?
is everyone's eye on you?
do you receive special treatment? profuse care?
delicious seeds?

do not be fooled

fly out or feign death before you realize
you are only the miner's canary

your rosy paradise is only a rusty cage in the
intestines of a filthy mine

what do you look for in humans?
the snake's armpit?
the elephant's beard?
or the butterfly's penis?

i wish society had an emergency exit
one with an ice cream booth next to it

i will leave your town soon

i will disappear and have my name fade out of your
dirty mouths for good

i will leave you with your filthy words, thoughts,
and deeds

remember, i was never a part of this

in the world you have created, charity reaches the poor most effectively when left in the garbage

human groups are designed to connect through massive food waste piles,

and to communicate in the medium of leftovers and expired cans

enjoy the abstract art of dried pork blood on the garbage bag

that's the civilization you have created

the “uncivilized” kill each other
the “civilized” kill each other and kill the
“uncivilized”

oh how organized and effective your civil barbarism
is

you will kill us all
only to find
you will drown with us all

they accused the broken windowpane of murdering
the hailstones

they called it justice

listen to what they don't say

no train has ever stopped to nurse the sparrow it ran over

and no passenger seems to have heard its tweet in the train wheel's roar

… the historian knows how to present the blood stains as rail rust

look!
the scarecrows have rooted deep and far
they have conquered the land in the name of
"security"

listen!
in this age of paranoia
there is no difference between "truth" and "crow
call"

when heads are stuffed with straw
"chaos" is cawed as "calm"

it's the silence of the lambs

the republic of wolves does not function on intelligence

wolves can only rule when the lambs are silent

a little lamb was crying
it had fallen in love with the slaughterhouse boy

yes, look around you:

sheep are chanting their butchers' incantations in joy, and their soft tails' fat-bags dance around to the beat of the knife sharpener

either the miner’s canary,
or the scapegoat,
the elephant in the room,
the lion’s share,
or the dead horse

yes, i know my role
and i know yours: the bee's knees

who cares what the city's squares are called when
they're not yours?
'republic', 'people,' 'freedom'...

why would the name of a street sign matter when
your role is to sweep refuse after the parade?

or to mop university floors with walls that scream
'equity' and 'equality'?

words won't save you
the game is still the same
they bleach your words
you clean their shit

it was a mistake to imagine people would mind their
own business if i minded mine

I was their business
I was their dirty plan

so I made *them* my noble goal

if your bullets smash my chest red to silence my
voice, i will turn into garnet graffiti with my fist in
the air

if you attack me with your state-funded paint, i will
turn into a nursery rhyme and fly around poor kids'
pale pink anemic lips

if you censor children's books, i will find my way
into mothers' lamentations for their murdered kids
and make your sleep a crimson nightmare with
lightning howls

you thought you could tear me up by the roots
you are a fool
i crept into the lush jungles of my imagination
and used your shitty visions as manure to grow
invincible plants
i will survive

"see the glass half full" is a pathetic argument
i want it all
and I want it as full as the ocean
don't make me feel guilty because i'm thirsty!
we are talking about a glass of water
is that too much to ask?

to hell with your lantern
i have the Sun

the flood is coming and guess what
your umbrella won't save you

I

i'm a crow gazing at january through glass
kaleidoscopic eyes

winter has plans, grand and ignoble

i decide that winter cannot freeze me dead

i sit here and watch january's brutal grandeur, as it crystallizes all the life on earth

death is here all around me

i cry

the steam rising from my tears warms my head

pain heats

i'm frozen and the sun is rising
will i melt with the snow?
will my body sustain its form when the ice peels?

i feel like a calendar pinned on a prison wall

i mark each day with eyes misty of unattained
dissipating dreams

i'm a sheet of paper withering with unremovable
stains

look at me from afar

or my bitter facial lines will leave you feeling
unlearned

you are knocking in vain
i have left me
nobody's home!

my head is a suitcase on
a baggage claim conveyor belt
turning
turning
turning
the passenger has left it behind

it feels like my mind will never be tidy
all these flying bits and whirling pieces
my mind is a bankrupt merchant's warehouse

nothing! nothing frightens me anymore!
nothing scares the hell out of my guts
what has become of me?

suffocation
again.

which mass-stranding whale tribe do i belong to?
i haven't caused this mess
i shouldn't crumple on my own
will the tribe die with me?

i will leave
i will pull my name out of the world's mouth
pack it in the silence of my suitcase, and leave

i left my home with a naive plan: leave the ruins
behind

alas, the ruins are inside me
wherever I go, I look inside and hurt

i close my eyes: all I see is debris
i open my eyes: all I see is dust

i carry my body around as an everyday obligation
in their company, i put a polite smile on

i pretend that with every step, a part of my flesh is
not decaying
that with every breath, a piece of my heart is not
rotting

i keep being polite because they are always around

no, you can never be alone in this jungle of
loneliness

my role in the last lovemaking i took part in:
the winning sperm in my parents' egg race

my role in your world's rat race:
another loser heading to his bed of loneliness with
just enough money to pay the bills

someday soon
the ants in my room
will devour my wi-fi and carry me to the garden
on their backs

they will do that someday
someday soon

i've made friends with two ants

at night, we quietly hang around the garden pond
until morning

the empty pond looks like a grave

as we get ready to lie down in the pond, we debate
who might bring flowers for our grave

we laugh and run towards the orange trees

the ants are careful not to step on me

since you left, i've become an art lover:

i peruse paintings to relocate your colors

listen to every note, searching for the waves of your
voice

i walk around downtown statues towering above
our favorite ice cream booths to savor the remains
of your presence

You

i'm still here, waiting for you like a deserted castle
i'm dusted with the memory of your stormy attack
how you conquered my soul!
wild neighs and hoof beats swirl in my cold towers
... still.

yes, with the same smile ... that same sweet smile …
you have slashed hearts, lashed hopes, and gashed
memories … with the same nightmarish sweetness

your one-night stand was my One Thousand and
One Nights

my love for you is as everlasting as a plastic bag
it'll remain around for thousands of years
it will outlive your garden's trees and your children's dreams

this sick
plastic
love

if you had joined me,
plastic wouldn't have been invented
trees wouldn't disappear
and children's dreams would come true

has our separation become one of those festive traditions that pleasure the powerful and burn the oppressed?

because it's night again and i'm going to bed, withering

and you, yes you, my butterfly, you're flying around the garden whispering your sweetness into smiling blossoms and swinging plants

you are a rivulet flowing towards nothingness
enjoy your winding journey!

what i fear more than the half-packed luggage in the
corridor

is the roads you tour and detour, build and null in
your imagination

deep down i know i will never be part of your
journey

whether or not you leave me, what i fear most is the
maps in your head

and you will forget me nonchalantly

like you forget small talk with an exhausted barista

and you will have me feeling as lonely as a city
dandelion on a windy day downtown

could i temper the sorrow caused by this
separation?

if at least I knew how many cities are between us
what do they call you now? an immigrant? alien?

one of these days, i'll disappear into a VHS-quality
video and chase you in pre-industrial woods and
you will run around through the trees and the
scratches of the Old Movie effect

your smell is in my breath; your breath is in my thoughts; my thoughts are in your hair; your hair is the clouds; the clouds are in my head; you are a cloud in my head; you never left; you're always raining in me; and i always smell of the rain in your hair.

come closer and see the marks of your absences
the burns and bruises
no, nobody can kiss them away
but we might happen to kiss again to remember

have you ever seen a singing cloud? those that sob
with a heavy, gloomy lump in their hearts?

my girl's hair is made of those clouds, and so are my
eyes

all I can see are dark lyrical curves

you are a pomegranate wrapped tight in your secret
swollen truth seeds

inside your sealed existence, invisible cracks are
growing

sooner or later, your cheeks will be stained red,
bleeding with expression

there are ten people in me
and you can see only one:

one human maintaining a measured conversation
with you over this cup of tea

the other eight are composing poems for your
beauty

and the tenth is playing the trumpet in a nearby
basement

enough, i am not
not enough to love you
there should be more of me
to comprehend your beauty
i need to multiply
i need to become a circle of poets, painters,
musicians, and mystics

i am jealous of your dress
it gets to rest in the aroma of your bosom
self-indulgently
no, there is no justice in the world!

i have a plan

i'll evaporate into an aromatic thought and
penetrate your daydream
while you are on
your 15-minute lunch break on minimum wage
while exhaustion steals your concentration

you and the bureaucracy of your love
every day a new Emotions Report Form

a missing tick on the form boxes,
a meeting,
a cancellation,
an additional signature needed.
communication issues
internet shutdowns
and when the submission is complete
your "tomorrow, tomorrow, tomorrow..."

it's getting late
the decision should be made now

"let's play hide and seek"

"sure, one condition only: i'll kiss your cheek if i find you"

"deal, [whispering in fear] i'll be lying in the rose garden"

my immortal blues bleed to a colorful death when
your rainbow smile rises above the pathetic battle of
daily survival

smile, speak, sip, sigh, smoke
the movement of your lips is the impetus of the universe

centuries of philosophizing
and your eyes mess up all speculations in a split
second

look! no don't look! no, don't! don't look!
here we go again

with eyelashes like swords
the less you blink, the more i get to see your eyes
the more you blink, the closer i am to death
they slice my heart with every flutter
hurry, just finish me already
i'd rather die than not see your eyes

i am not a poet
i am a reporter
i just report your eyes

the coup d'état of your rose lip rouge
the police dogs of your eyes
and again, you throw me behind your eyelashes'
cage bars
where are my human rights?

the storm in your hair locks and the tornado of
your eyelashes

those furious black waves, those roaring dark rivers

how many broken ships? how many evaporated
visions, expired charts, antique logs?

how many souls shattered on your rugged rocky
beauty?

give me a number

i need to make sure i haven't been your only victim

that would be the only relief

what do you mix with your voice that kills all my demons? let's keep talking!

lost in your orange imagination

i drink the night with all its seeds, pulp, and bubbles

you imagine a revolution; i bleed on tarmac

you picture a dance; I become a black beauty mark
on your rosy cheek

this dance will take two

It

Hope is the opium of the oppressed.

Joy? I left it behind in my mother's muddy
vegetable garden when I walked into the world.

Breaking News is only latter-day fire-eating
what a performance! don't fall for it
nothing has changed
the world is the same filthy hole
the only difference: you've become numb
you are a drunk spectator's eye,
decoding a fire eater's flame-calligraphy on the grey
sky

did you know “Human” is a swear word among
animals

and the name of a poisonous weed among trees?

Life is a frothy dream in the broken crest of a
stormy ocean wave

Life is the balloon in a toddler's hand on a windy day

Fate is a colorful, emotional butterfly
Fate softly perches on your shoulder
with all its poignant pigments
and flutters away in a flash
so quickly that you can't sense the color that will
forever stain your life

yes, Life is a butterfly roulette with different shades
of blade

Time can bend
yes, i have touched Time

years have passed

but what broke in my heart, still gongs in my head,
and tears all my joints

Time never heals

ants are carrying the decayed corpse of my dreams
in broken bits, and i'm watching them through a
numb blurry indifference

no, this depression is not a wild wolf howling
it's a slow and deliberate one-thousand-tentacled
octopus

the surrealism of everyday life's realism: how exciting! how scary!

our apartment is shrinking
the walls are aggressively closing in on us
these four concrete panels will kill us soon
let's close our eyes and think of rice paddies
let's close our eyes and get our feet wet with the
water around the rice plants of our imagination

sometimes it's only Imagination that can liberate

the party was in full swing
the room crowded with dancing limbs
hungry, i saw the mango on a small coffee table in
the corner of the room

between us though
stood police dogs,
pepper spray,
torture manuals,
refugee camps.

i felt as though I could never reach the mango
i had another drink

neither Death is so bitter
nor Life so sweet

there are better things like
mangoes
ice cream cones
or colorful bean bag chairs

if Coffee was a human
i'd make love to it at every sunset
when all colors mix and my pores are ready to
embrace all shades of cream

in my Loneliness, i've read books
in all the sex positions you can imagine.

your Twilight is ready!
would you like some cream in it? sugar?

the loyalty of a Candle

dances when you're joyful
cries when you are sad

speak Lady Ocean
whisper your wet wisdom
let the breeze wrap and carry your words

my Heart is falling apart like a fisherman's torn net

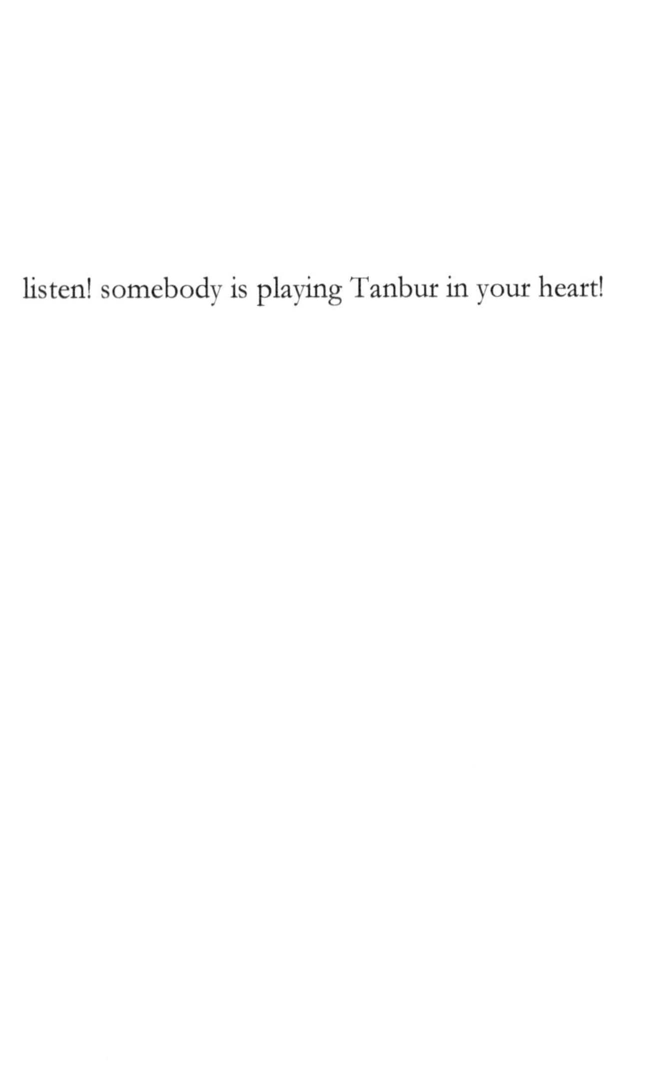

listen! somebody is playing Tanbur in your heart!

in my heart, a Cow is giving birth and villagers are shouting in my veins!

Love is fire
and lovers: fire feeders

be careful with our love
for it can warm up our lives
or burn our house down

"LOVE" has only four letters but it's a one-thousand-page saga which burns like an epic and hurts like a tragedy!

to love is to paint
and painting is not only to layer colors on canvas
but also to remove paint and to reveal shades
to blur lines and to hide shapes

The Nightingale was bruised, her eyes bleeding
she was singing lamentations of love
she had fallen in love with her butcher

The Fallen Tree was lamenting
"who axed you down?"
"the man who rested in my shade"

to dream, or to look naked reality in the eye, that is
the question

whether to indulge in imagining, when you are
down, beaten and broken

or to dream dreams that will never come true

to drift from illusion to illusion, mirage to mirage

isn't there a fine line between imagination and
hallucination?

can an illusioned slave ever be free?

and don’t forget
Hopelessness can liberate, also!

don't expect flavor from Water
Water is essential
dream-free and bland

you want to see the Light
then, turn it on!

i need a colossal Scrub to cleanse the world
and loud battle songs to wash out my brain dregs
and unclog my veins

He

there has been no rain in years, and still all the roofs
are dripping

we pretend it's a miracle gifted by a god

but everybody knows that the youth in our town cry
blood-tears in their confinement

yes, all these red drops.

God should have stopped at plants and animals
creating humans was a grave miscalculation
a short-sighted error
a fatal mistake

God, you'd better pray that you're a figment of
human's Imagination
otherwise on the Day of Judgment
i'll make you pay for your incompetence

who knows? God might be another rich snob with
lots of stupid ideas

God is a bad dramatist who keeps confusing
"comic relief" with "tragedy"

carelessly using *deus ex machina* when his plots fail

and ending each act with nonsensical conclusions as
soon as he feels bored with writing

God is Satan's invention
a gift for humans to survive the world's evil with
the illusion of godly goodness
goodies for goofs and gagas

God is the tacky halo around Satan's head
the more faithful you are, the deeper your bow
against evil

flood, bombs, blood, drought, tears, torn, tornado,
volcano, quake, wave, lamed, underfed, fatigue,
famine, mean…seems like God is in need of some
meditation—or at least a couple of tranquilizers

what a great variety of dishes!
we'll have two poverty lines please
one medium, one well-done

do not rush! your turn will come soon!

He is a deliberate monster with a detailed plan to
devour us one by one

the feast is long, and he is starving

do not rush! your turn will come soon!

oh, i just remembered
we are all going to die

We

there are things you cannot do on your own
things like Romance and Revolution

there are no rules in war
nor in love
so play hard!

with ten thousand people: loneliness
without ten thousand people: loneliness
oh, this ten-thousand-year-old loneliness

you'll get used to your cocoon soon
just listen to the butterflies' laments

when you realize you're nothing but another impression for social media ads and propaganda posts, you'll decide that you'll have to love. love! love savagely! with no consideration. no calculation.

when you are the wall, speaking of liberation is
either delusional or hypocritical

what keeps you away
is you
not the prison

no, you aren't afraid of heights
you're afraid of flight, of freedom

the train of certainty hasn't left the station yet. we are a flash mob performing "doubt" for the punctual wax passengers and filling their lead suitcases with cotton candies.

a furious night is barbarically falling over the city
and there isn't much I can do

"should I keep my eyes open or close them not to
see the tragedy?"

sometimes even blinking is a political act

the crisis in this house is ongoing
the official reports are propaganda popcorn
the only reliable source of information:
late-night tears

if we cry together:
a flood

beware! there is no victory in this game!
we are gambling against the night
the more we win, the murkier we get
all we can get from night is night

you will die at forty-five with the arrows that you
shot when you were twenty

you will die as you watch your shooting dreams
disappear in the cloudy skies of your life

with a small puff here and a quiet spark there

then, you start to vote for the lesser evil

you will soon be old enough to see
that every side loses
it's just a matter of time
some sooner, some later

no, i'm not crying
i'm just watering a few withering memories

all that is behind is ruins
and all that is ahead is a mirage
you are a story in between
tell yourself while there is still time

enduring such a deep wet wound
gives us an advantage
we don't fall dead in blank horror
we can swim the length of a long death
in a numb daze
and imagine colorful futures,
floating on bloody shades of dewy red

i saw it in her eyes
her eyes had seen the catastrophe
the choice for me now was
either to focus on her eyes
or on the catastrophe

our planet does not need powerful men
we need lovers, healers, and storytellers

i am looking for someone to waste my time with
isn't that a form of activism?

how often do you turn your world upside down?

the liberator is in the mirror

and the tyrant: the dust on the glass

"There are things you cannot do on your own; things like Romance and Revolution": Tweets of Love and Protest

Social media platforms generate textual content that can be treated as data, offering some unfiltered information about how citizens regard themselves in relation to states and how they organize to resist repressive governments. Social media such as X, which at the time of conducting this project was called Twitter, allow the appearance of voices traditionally invisible in mainstream cultural and discursive interactions. They have a "carnivalesque" character that permits diverse participation of people and manners, that "has a universal spirit; it is a special condition of the entire world, of the world's revival and renewal, in which all [people regardless of their social status] take part" (Bakhtin, 1981, p. 7). As a result of this authorial diversity and rhetorical flexibility, texts shared on social media can provide researchers with greater access to the emotional expressions of individuals who participate in or witness social movements.

Interested in this potential, in this section of the book, I focus on social media posts shared during a series of protests in Iran that arose between December 2017 to May 2022 and were crushed by the government. I conducted this project to better understand how people involved in social movements emotionally react to political events. The poems that you read in the previous section are the outcome of collecting and analyzing a pool of about 2,000 tweets in Farsi that carried Iranian protesters' emotional expressions about and reactions to the crackdown against the protests. I translated some of these tweets from Farsi into English and reconstructed them to frame a poetic narrative that can provide more understanding of the dynamics of social movements and civil resistance through the emotional landscape of protesters and people who witnessed these recurring protests.

Although the Iran protests eventually attracted some attention in the West by culminating in the Woman, Life, Freedom Movement in 2022 and the current massive 2026 protests, the violent crackdowns on the uprisings between December 2017 and May 2022 were met with silence from the media, Western politicians, and international institutions. The world's silence about this violence created much outrage among the Iranians. This poetic inquiry was an attempt to unearth non-trending tweets from the periods between the crackdowns to bring some visibility to the emotional status of the protesters and the people who witnessed the crackdowns. In this section, after describing the context of the project and the inquiry approach, I discuss how the poems that I have curated in this book depict the protesters' emotional world and what their emotional expressions can tell us about the dynamics of anti-oppressive social movements.

Context

The current government in Iran is an Islamic republic. It is a theocratic republic ruled by Shia clerics who—up until their current face-off with the United States and the possibility of war as I type these words—have made cosmetic use of liberal democratic features such as parliamentary and presidential elections to appeal to Western observers and sustain semi-normal economic relations with the world. Over the past decades, they also engaged in economic activities such as privatizing public services and following World Bank policies in order to be welcomed by Western institutions and networks that run the neoliberal global markets. Since its establishment in the wake of the Iranian Revolution in 1979, the Islamic Republic has had serious issues with legitimizing its rule as a result of its overt violent confrontation with opposition forces, systematic persecution of dissidents, and disregard for women's rights.

Collective dissatisfaction with the Islamic Republic has resulted in many social movements regularly crushed by the regime's violent response. Examples include: the crushing of women's protests against the regime's mandatory veiling laws in 1979; the execution of political opposition members in the 1980s (estimated to exceed 30,000 people); the "chain murders" of Iranian intellectuals, journalists, and writers in the 1990s; the oppression of the student protests of July 1999; and the killing and detaining of Green Movement demonstrators in 2009 and 2010; the violent suppression of the Woman, Life, Freedom movement in 2022; and the ongoing massacre of thousands of 2026 protesters.

The Islamic Republic has constantly generated new waves of protests as a result of policies that have led to inflation, a devalued currency, a shrinking middle class, unemployment, housing crises, and environmental damage such as the desertification of the country due to mismanagement of water resources. In response, in the past decade, students, teachers, nurses, farmers, factory workers, truck drivers, women, and retirees have staged small and large protests in different parts of the country. Three major uprisings—before the Woman, Life, Freedom movement in 2022 and the 2026 protests—that challenged the Islamic Republic existentially (Shahi & Abdoh-Tabrizi, 2020) were: the mass protests of December 2017, November 2019, and May 2022. As confirmed by Reuters, at least 1,500 protesters were killed in the 2019 protests alone, which has earned the name "Bloody November" in public discourse. As a result of systematic censorship inside the country and the Republic's exertion of influence on Farsi- and English-language media outside its borders, Twitter was the main venue for citizens, activists, and protesters to share information about the protests and to express their outrage in response to the Republic's violence (Grossman, 2009; Hashemi et al., 2022).

Although the Iranian protesters, and their allies and supporters, were active on Twitter during the Bloody November massacre, they did not manage to break through the international silence about the regime's atrocities. Also, because they mostly tweeted in Farsi, their hashtag campaigns hardly became viral on English Twitter. This project is an attempt to bring visibility to this body of text, which has been largely ignored because of language difference and, sadly, lack of interest on the part of international political observers. The title of the collection of poems, *Thus Twote Zarathustra*, is a tongue-in-cheek reference to Nietzsche's *Thus Spoke Zarathustra*. This title is meant to highlight that when Iranian traditions are viewed as oriental objects of the past, they are idolized by Western thinkers, but contemporary Iranians' voices remain unheard and are deemed insignificant. *Thus Twote Zarathustra* is intended to share some of the profundity of the collective thoughts of today's ordinary Iranians.

At the same time, this project is a contribution to a growing pool of research projects that focus on Farsi Twitter as a source of data about Iranians' perceptions of the recurring uprisings (see for instance, Azadi & Mesgaran, 2021; Burns & Eltham, 2009; Kermani & Adham, 2021; Morozov, 2009; Shayesteh & Seo, 2022). In the process of this inquiry, I specifically looked for tweets that captured Iranians' emotional reactions to the protests during the period in question. Interested in emotional expression as political praxis, I explored ordinary citizens' Twitter posts, rather than journalists' or political activists' tweets, to discover how the people's emotional status reflected the political developments in the streets.

In this prose component of the book, I provide analyses of the poems through the lens of "textual production as socio-political performance." Here I offer a discussion about the poems, guided by the following questions: What can these poems tell us about the emotional world of protesters and the way they imagined themselves in relation to political events? What can we learn about social movements and their dynamics by studying emotional expressions in response to protests, especially after violent crackdowns? How can poetic inquiry help reframe non-trending social media posts as creative and intellectual expression, and thus provide them with more visibility?

Emotion as Politics

In this project, I drew on two theoretical frameworks: *passionate politics* and *sociological imagination. Passionate politics* (Goodwin et al., 2001) is an umbrella concept that highlights discourses that are interested in emotive reactions to, and emotional involvement in, social movements. Exploring passionate politics is an attempt at "reincorporating emotions such as anger and indignation, fear and disgust, joy and love, into research on politics and protest. Emotions, properly understood, may prove once again to be a central concern of political analysis" (Goodwin et al., 2001, p. 3). In what follows, I focus on the connection between affect and politics in order to discuss how the emotional expressions, shared as the above poems, host meanings that can help us better understand the dynamics of social movements and the human interactions that form protests.

If emotions are a significant component of social movements, protesters' online emotional expressions on platforms such as Twitter can be treated as an important source of data for understanding activists' *sociological imagination* (Mills, 1959). Sociological imagination is "a source of empowerment for ordinary people. It allow[s] them to see themselves autobiographically – as historical actors both shaped by and shaping history" (Mukerji, 2018, p. 119). It also pushes back against the state's narrative of what a nation wants to be to reveal ordinary people's and their communities' visions of their futures. Sociological imagination "is a good means for querying the silent political habitus of things established by states that has silently and relentlessly eroded the ability of people to dream of change, because it addresses dreams of possibility in a different way than states" (Mukerji, 2018, p. 119).

Accordingly, this project has been intended to create a narrative of the protests through the emotional eye of the protesters. In this project, I have brought together isolated tweets to frame them as a brief emotional history of the said protests. Although these tweets are personal reflections and expressions of individual feelings, they mirror sociopolitical developments. They help us see how emotions have been a significant part of the ongoing protests in Iran and how emotive expressions function as a means of imagining alternative futures.

Feel of the Field

Papacharissi's work (2002, 2010) has successfully established an area of communication studies that specifically focuses on new media, especially the internet, as a social space. In her work, she shows that "new technologies provide information and tools that may extend the role of the public in the social and political arena" (Papacharissi, 2002, p. 10). Furthermore, she underlines the connection between affect and digital politics: "Affect is inherently political. It provides a way of understanding humans as collective and emotional, as well as individual and rational, by presenting these states as confluent rather than opposite" (Papacharissi, 2015, p. 16).

Park (2013), similarly, has written about Twitter as a new participatory culture that contributes to a political carnivalism that should be studied for a better understanding of current political climates in different contexts. In the same line of scholarship, Rodríguez (2019) has highlighted the importance of *technopolitics* and citizen use of digital media. The political significance of the new media also has theoretical overlap with Downing's (2014) conceptualization of *nano-media*, which explains how small media connect with social movements. Nano-media are small-scale media that can provide alternative grassroots narratives to mass media's mainstream conceptualizations of social affairs. Nano-media can also act as a means of community building and organizing social action.

Social media has been frequently discussed as a means of political participation (Effing, 2011; Halpern, 2017; Saldaña et al., 2015). In this literature, however, there is a trend that specifically focuses on social media as a space for *expression*, which is more in line with the content of the project that this book is based on. For instance, Gil de Zúñiga (2018) writes:

> It has been argued that social media can facilitate political expression, a crucial alley for people to get engaged in politics (Pingree, 2007) … social media as a user-friendly platform cultivates political consciousness of users in their daily practice, therefore is believed to display political expression in a more accessible format and spirited condition, ultimately facilitating expression and participation." (p. 1174)

In this sense, social media provide alternative forms

of communicating political views to the traditional formats offered by public tribunes, television, radio, and the press. Social media, in particular, create a rare genre space for less regulated political expressions such as emotional reactions to political developments. An emphasis on emotions, as a mirror to one's inner self as well as to the political, can help us see social media posts as "political self-concepts": "Political self-concepts may be considered a collection of perceptions about one's role, competence, and engagement in politics. … A political self-concept captures the extent to which a person thinks of themselves as a "political person"" (Lane et al., 2019, p. 51). From this perspective, writing about emotions, and the ability to instantly share posts publicly, can render emotional expression as political activism by the mere act of making one's emotions about social movements visible.

The potential of Twitter to bring together minoritized communities, vulnerable citizens, social critics, and political dissidents has already attracted the attention of researchers from different disciplines. For instance, Brock (2012) used critical race theory and technocultural theory to study Black users' treatment of Twitter as a venue for civic activism. Williams (2015) studied how Black women and girls used Twitter to bring attention to Black women's issues and concerns, long ignored by traditional mainstream media. In an edited volume about Indigenous peoples' social media activism, Carlson and Frazer (2021) studied expressions of anger, hope, and love in response to Twitter hashtags significant in Indigenous social and political movements. Siapera et al. (2018) also focused on affective expressions on Twitter in their analysis of 7.5 million tweets during the refugee crisis between October 2015 and May 2016, tracking the movement of asylum seekers from the Middle East and Africa to Europe. Discussing their findings, they show that "affective publics on Twitter typically produce disruptions/interruptions of dominant narratives" (p. 3). In a project that explored Indian feminists' use of Twitter in their activism, Losh (2014) highlighted the significance of the emotional and affective labor that women of color invest in political causes. Wonneberger et al. (2021) analyzed Dutch animal welfare debates on Twitter to study how microblogging can contribute to the configuration of counterpublics, or parallel discursive spaces that allow the creation and circulation of counter discourses. They found that emotional load is a feature of Twitter activism. Keller et al. (2018) documented women's Twitter responses to rape culture with a special interest in exploring the affective experiences of the people who engaged with this content. They found emotions to be an essential component of these debates with expressions of "shock, disgust, fear, panic and anger" (p. 27). With the same focus on rape culture and everyday sexism, Phipps et al. (2018) explored how the personal affect expressed on Twitter facilitated an affective connectivity that could be used as political capital. Nau et al. (2022), also, have reported that vernacular practices, such as using euphemisms, emojis, and indirect participation, on #MeToo Twitter facilitated expression of emotions as a key part of the movement.

Analyzing words with affective connotations on Twitter, Tsugawa et al. (2015) suggest that it is possible to identify individuals who are struggling with depression and anxiety on Twitter because social media open up space for emotional expressions. Wang and Wei (2020) discussed how the cancer community use Twitter to share their emotions. They reported that the cancer-affected population shared feelings of joy and hope as well as sadness, fear, and anger. This finding challenges simplifications of the range of emotions that cancer survivors have lived with. In another project that explored emotional reactions to the COVID-19 pandemic, Xue et al. (2020) showed that emotional expressions about confirmed cases and deaths over time changed from questions about trust to expressions of fear.

The present project contributes to this body of research by focusing on political dimensions of emotional expression on Twitter in the context of Iranian protests. What significantly distinguishes this inquiry from the projects listed above is its methodological approach, which I discuss next.

Poetic Inquiry as Praxis: Reclaiming Voice from the Margins

Poetic inquiry is a form of arts-based research that, through creative rendering and reconstruction of data, explores complex meanings in text (Faulkner, 2017; Galvin & Prendergast, 2012; Prendergast et al., 2009; Thomas et al., 2012). Poetic inquiry allows researchers to use the potentials of poetic lyricism and imagery as an epistemological tool to discover and reveal the complexities of phenomena. "Poetic inquiry is a way of knowing through poetic language and devices; metaphor, lyric, rhythm, imagery, emotion, attention, wide-awakeness, opening to the world, self-revelation" (Prendergast, 2009, p. xxxvii). "Poetic inquiry is the use of poetry as/in/for inquiry" (Faulkner, 2017, p. 210); thus, in this form of research, poetry can be used as part of (in/for) or the whole project (as). In my project, I used poetry as a form of analysis in the manner that I will detail below.

1- I collected about 2,000 Farsi tweets shared during the mass protests of December 2017, November 2019, May 2022, and the periods between them. I specifically looked for tweets that contained emotional expressions by Iranians who witnessed or participated in the protests. With a focus on the relationship between affect and social movements, I avoided collecting tweets with direct political messages or demands in the initial phase of data collection. Thus, I ignored tweets by journalists or political activists and tried to focus on ordinary citizens' affective expressions. Focusing on these non-trending expressions of emotion would also allow bypassing posts by Twitter bots whenever possible.

2- I conducted a thematic analysis of these tweets to identify common themes that could help me make sense of current politics through emotional expressions such as anger, depression, loneliness, fear, and love. Guided by my research questions, I wanted to see whether citizens' emotions could reveal information about the political status of the country and the dynamics of the ongoing social movement.

3- After identifying the major themes, I organized them in an order that could best frame the tweets within a narrative reflecting and explaining some of the dynamics of the ongoing protests. As I will illustrate later, the narrative has been structured around the following themes: oppression, alienation, recovery, romance, and revolution.

4- From the initial 2,000 tweets, I selected about 200 representative tweets that could sustain the aforementioned narrative while also fitting within a document of manageable length. This selection process was guided by the vision of turning the Farsi tweets into English poems to be presented as a collection of poems. The poems curated in the book are based on these 200 tweets.

5- I translated the tweets into English while modifying them to resemble poems. This step was the main poetic analysis component of the project. In order to maximize meaning generation, I used poetic language in my analysis of the tweets to sharpen, exaggerate, imagize, metaphorize, tune, and tonify the emotions expressed, making the affective politics contained in the texts as visible as possible. In this process, I created poetry out of available texts by keeping the main content while adding poetic elements. I call my approach *refractive poetic analysis*. In this form of analysis, poetry is created by adding poetic components to the text under analysis to highlight and further construct its meanings. In the case of the current project, the translation process, in particular, allowed ample space for the poetic restoration of the tweets in my attempt to better crystallize meanings. Translation from one language to another creates multiple possibilities for representing the same meanings and, thus, invites the translator's creative involvement.

Butler-Kisber (2010) categorizes poetic inquiry approaches as "found poetry" and "generated poetry." In a found poetry project, poems are created from texts that already exist. In a generated poetry inquiry, participants or researchers generate poems (using their own words) either during the process of data collection or in the presentation of findings. Found poetry has been successfully used in inquiries that mobilize critical paradigms and focus on questions about identity. For example, Allen and Simon (2021) used found poetry in a Grade 8 class and asked students to create poetry from classical literary works such as *Fahrenheit 451* to see how students imagine reconstruing canonical texts. Dill et al. (2016) created erasure poems with lesbian, gay, and bisexual migrants in Johannesburg to study how non-binary migrants interacted and were received in their new context. Meyer (2008) asked pre-service teachers to create found poetry to make their evolving teacher identities visible. An Indigenous researcher, Metallic (2017) interviewed the Mi'gmaq adult learners in her heritage language class about their experiences learning their ancestors' language. She created found poems out of her interview transcripts to show how the students felt about learning a language almost lost. As an example of generated poetry, Furman (2004) wrote poems that contained his emotional responses to complex existential experiences such as anxiety, dread, illness, and death. In another example of generated poetry, Chan (2003) used poetry to study her emotions as a social work doctoral student. She used poetry both as an epistemological tool and also as a means of sustaining her well-being in a challenging context.

In my project, I employed a third approach by using a poetic analysis method that can be described as situated between generated and found poetry. In this approach, I created poetry as a form of analytic reflection on the data. In other words, I used poetry both to make sense of the data and to reveal its meaning through poetic language. Throughout this process, I remained committed to representing the tweets' original conceptual themes; however, I allowed myself to freely add poetic elements to the final product for greater effect. This intervention was also justified by the project's focus on emotions. I hoped that the added poetic features would make the affective component more visible or relatable. As a result of this approach, it is now impossible to determine whether the poems are mine or belong to the Farsi Twitter users who posted the original tweets. The present poems are, in most cases, significantly different from the original texts and should be read as my poetic analysis of the content of those initial tweets.

6- After drafting the poems, the poetic narrative created from the representative tweets was used as a blueprint for a second round of data collection on Farsi Twitter. This phase involved searching for Twitter campaigns, hashtags, and activists' tweets to help me test and tune the poetic findings for a more realistic representation of the protests. In the following sections, I present my poetic analysis, substantiated by evidence from the second round of data collection. I discuss the poetic findings with examples of the non-poetic data that contain the same themes.

This project, as previously explained, aimed to generate knowledge about social movements with a focus on emotional expressions in non-trending tweets posted as a healing mechanism. Poetic inquiry allowed for a more effective surfacing of the emotional load of the tweets. "Poetry has the capacity to clarify and magnify existence. Poetry may be thought of as the emotional microchip, in that it may serve as a compact repository for emotionally charged experiences" (Furman, 2004, p. 1). Hopefully, refractive poetic analysis has helped me magnify the voices of these everyday citizens by translating and reconstructing their words, and by framing their scattered digital expressions of emotion as a coherent narrative.

The Poetics of Emotional Response to Oppression

Farsi Twitter became the main hub for news sharing and political debate throughout the mass protests of December 2017, November 2019, and May 2022. The content I collected shows that tweets containing Iranians' emotional reactions to the protests were posted more frequently in the post-protest periods, particularly in the wake of the state's violent crackdowns. Focused on content that expressed affect, I identified the following thematic progression on Farsi Twitter before, during, and after a protest (see Figure 1):

Figure 1
Order of major themes

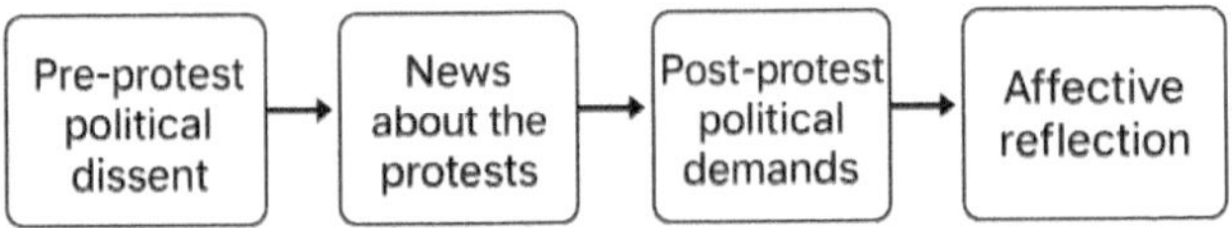

In the immediate pre-protest period, the tweets that dominated Farsi Twitter contained harsh criticisms of policies that had created socioeconomic and political problems such as the unbearable cost of living and aggressive oppression of women's rights. When the protests happened, Farsi Twitter predominantly engaged in sharing news and updates about the protesters on the ground. With street protests ending, Farsi Twitter typically entered a new phase in which the tweets stated specific political demands—such as urging opposition forces to unite, calling for the overthrow of the regime, and planning to reach out to international institutions to report the state's aggressions. Alongside these demands, the tweets continued echoing the chants of the protesters, often in the form of hashtags. The users also shared statements released by detained or murdered protesters' family members.

It was mainly in longer periods between major street protests that more reflective and affective tweets became visible. These were often periods when the protests had been crushed and the images of murdered protesters circulated on Farsi Twitter, usually depicting them in their everyday lives before the events. This stage turned into a period of digital mourning and deep reflection about the recent collective act of resistance aborted by the Republic.

Samples 1 and 2 show Farsi Twitter users' awareness of this stage as a period of post-protest depression and loneliness.

Sample 1 (Translation: *We have all entered the period of depression and anxiety that follows oppression and killings.*)

Sample 2 (Translation: *The days following the oppression of the #nationwide_protests are days of absolute loneliness for the detained protesters and their families... days and nights of loneliness, mourning, and desperation ...*)

The tweets that inspired the poems are from the final phase of each protest cycle. In the following sections, I discuss the narrative that I have used to frame the individual tweets collected for this project as a coherent totality. This narrative is by no means the only possible arrangement of these online expressions, but rather one of many potential interpretations. In this narrative, I have used the flexibilities bestowed by poetic inquiry to position myself as a poet-researcher within the less-heard voices of Farsi Twitter to provide an interpretation of the tweets that can explain some aspects of the relationship between human emotions and social movements. In harmony with the headings in the section that curated the poems, I discuss the poems in the following sequence: They → I → You → It → He → We.

In the section with the subheading "They," I explain how some of the tweets that I collected illustrate sentiments that describe the nature of the oppressive force that the people constantly face in the Islamic Republic. In "I," I focus on tweets that describe the alienation and loneliness experienced as a result of the oppression sustained and imposed by "They," the oppressive force. People, however, always seek a way out of their loneliness. Feelings of depression can be redeemed by reunification with "You": beloveds, companions, partners, and comrades who allow the growth of communities of resistance. In "You," I highlight the protesters' desire to come together. "It" contains a discussion of tweets portraying everyday objects that represent some of the protesters' emotions; "It," also, hosts descriptions of the instruments of the revolution. An extension of "It" is "He" or the religiosity that becomes another tool of oppression. "He" is also a personification of "They," serving as a thematic recall just before the final section, "We," to remind readers of the oppressive force that has rendered revolutionary action unavoidable. The final section is "We." "We" is the reunification of "I" and "You" as protesters move away from feelings of fear and anxiety. "We" represents rekindled hope for the possibility of reconstructing communities of protest for future uprisings and, thus, transformation.

"They": The Oppressive Apparatus and the Silence of the Oppressed

One major group of the tweets was texts that attempted to describe the oppressors and the nature of the oppression. When protests are brutally oppressed, it is only rational to ask who the oppressors are, how they function, and what strategies they employ. Here is a representative response:

> *the republic of wolves does not function on intelligence / wolves can only rule when the lambs are silent*

What enables the oppressive machine is a "republic of wolves" that thrives on violence. There is no intelligent strategy or sophisticated plan. The rulers of the Republic are "butchers" whose main political activity is "knife-sharpening":

> *yes, look around you / sheep are chanting their butchers' incantations in joy / and their soft tails' fat-bags dance around to the beat of the knife sharpener*

The tweets, as these poetic renditions show, are blunt

in their conceptualization of the character of the state. There is no ambiguity that the Republic thrives on displays of bare violence. The complexity, however, lies in the fact that any description of "They" as "violent rulers" appears together with another "They": groups of the oppressed who, ironically, have decided to support the Republic either through "silence" or the naive "joy" of being part of a herd: "*wolves only can rule when the lambs are silent.*" "*sheep are chanting their butchers' incantations in joy and tears.*" The first group of tweets are as much about the oppressive elite as they are about the silence of the oppressed. The oppressor is the enemy, and so is the obedient oppressed.

This poetic visualization of the relationship between the oppressor and the oppressed is not an obscure theme on Farsi Twitter. The hashtag #سندروم_استکهلم [#Stockholm_syndrome] is frequently employed when protests occur. "The term Stockholm syndrome has been used to describe the positive emotional bond a kidnap victim may develop towards their captor" (Namnyak et al., 2008, p. 1) as a survival strategy.

Deeper analysis of Farsi Twitter's description of Stockholm syndrome reveals that Iranian Twitter users see a connection between silence and economic class. Most of the protests between December 2017 and May 2022 were staged by provincial and rural factory and agricultural workers. The protests were also attended by unemployed youth living in industrial suburbs, as well as poor retirees. The tweets that highlight Stockholm syndrome often have a clear target: the middle class located in the affluent areas of the capital, Tehran. The behavior of this population is rather paradoxical because, in contrast with the conservative government, the Iranian middle class is often educated, progressive, and even West-leaning. However, this paradoxical bond between the middle class and the government has an economic explanation. The middle class has decided to sustain the status quo, which provides them with economic and cultural dominance. Before the 2022 Women, Life, Freedom movement and the 2026 protests, which also attracted the middle class, Farsi Twitter was sharply critical of the passivity of the middle class, especially in the capital, Tehran. See the following examples:

Sample 3 (Translation: *Most Iranians are aware that the Islamic Republic is our enemy, so why won't things change? We need to make the people in Tehran aware of Stockholm syndrome and discuss ways to give them courage.*)

Sample 4 (Translation: *Years later, they write that Stockholm syndrome is the older name for Tehran syndrome.*)

Sample 5 (Translation: … *People are suffering from Stockholm syndrome because they have gotten used to the systemic administrative corruption, among other forms of corruption* … .)

Under the pressure of public opinion, the capital's middle class often felt that they needed to provide an explanation for their passivity and indifference. Echoing the argument of the state, the middle class often mobilized a rhetoric around "security" to explain their lack of participation. The state frequently listed examples of the region's failed states, such as Syria, Yemen, and Afghanistan, to argue that any change to the current situation would lead to the destruction and disintegration of the country. Through state-run media, planted celebrities, and funded academics, the Republic manufactured a discourse that claimed whatever was lacking in the country, the state was successful in providing national security. In response, this rhetoric of "security" is often deconstructed on Farsi Twitter:

> *look! / the scarecrows have rooted deep and far / they have conquered the land in the name of "security" / listen! / in this age of paranoia / there is no difference between "truth" and "crow call" / when rationality is stuffed with straw / "chaos" is cawed as "calm"*

The message in this poem is echoed in hundreds of sarcastic tweets that mock the use of the expression "at least we have security" to justify the everyday violation of human rights. Here are some examples:

Sample 6 (Translation: *The pizza that was 95,000 toman last week is 175,000 toman today. Instead, we have security? What kind of security is this? …)*

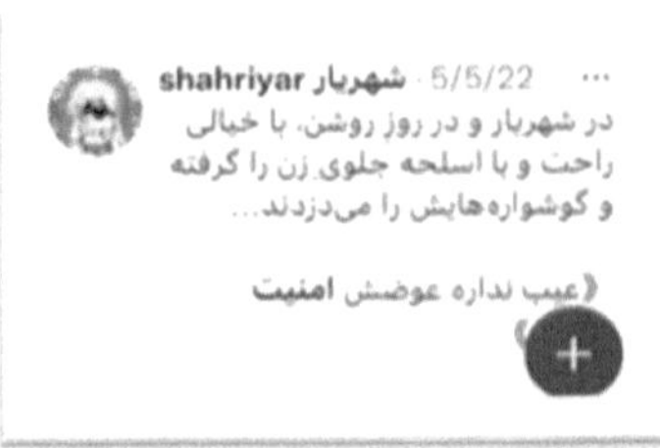

Sample 7 (Translation: … *In broad daylight, they comfortably mugged a woman and stole her earrings. 'No worries. At least we have security".*)

Sample 8 (Translation: … *They kill the people who protest because of the price of bread, and, of course, "thank God, we have security."*)

Creating the rhetoric of "security" requires the participation of the intellectual elite:

> *no train has ever stopped to nurse the sparrow it ran over / and no passenger seems to have heard its tweet in the train wheel's roar / … the historian knows how to present the blood stains as rail rust*

As the use of the word "historian" in this poem indicates, journalists and academics, as an important sector of the middle class, are hard at work fabricating a narrative that hides the state's crimes by representing "blood" as "rust." The "train" that has kept us "secure" moves forward, and the life of a little sparrow is only a small price. Why bring the attention of the public to it? My reference to funded intellectuals is not entirely based on my interpretation of this poem. There is a lot of sensitivity on Farsi Twitter about the role of the funded intelligentsia and their collaboration with the oppressors.

For instance, the color-based metaphor in this poem, the redness of "blood," reminds one of a commonly used hashtag on Farsi Twitter: #نون_در_خون or #bread_in_blood. To dip one's bread in people's blood connotes earning a livelihood that is sustained by a condition that causes the death of other people. Farsi Twitter activists used the #bread_in_blood hashtag to tweet at people who normalized the state's behavior because their public influence and income were tied to the Islamic Republic's cultural and political hegemony. Farsi Twitter immediately expressed outrage at any reaction to the state's treatment of the protests that failed to address the brutality comfortably waged by the regime. Here is a tweet in response to the elite's call for participation in the regime's engineered elections:

Sample 9 (Translation: *Participation in the elections means approval of the behavior of the Islamic Republic. Participation in the elections means shooting our children [young protesters]. Participation in the elections means dipping your bread in the blood of Iranians.*)

Farsi Twitter was aware that oppression does not breed security, but imprisonment, torture, and death. State aggression might provide security for a certain class whose economic existence is tied to the state's behavior. Nevertheless, this security might be only temporary. Farsi Twitter activists reminded the silent middle class that the Islamic Republic has a history of eliminating its own allies when the system does not need them, and that they are merely the miner's canary, intended to die first if the mine becomes poisonous:

> *do they spoil you? / does everyone love you? / is everyone's eye on you? / do you receive special treatment? profuse care? delicious seeds? / do not be fooled / fly out or feign death before you realize you are the miner's canary / your rosy paradise is only a rusty cage in the intestines of a filthy mine*

Eventually, we will all be victims. The machine will crush us all because that is the only function of the machine. You might be the next victim:

> *a little lamb was crying / it had fallen in love with the slaughterhouse boy*

If you feel there is security, it is because you are still part of the machine, and thus, you have not heard the voices of the people who were crushed by it.

Hence, one interpretation of the major themes in the "They" poems can be Farsi Twitter users' characterization of the nature of the ongoing oppression as brute aggression. Moreover, they lead us to recognize that besides the state, collaborators and bystanders are, willing or unwillingly, part of the problem. In the period prior to the Woman, Life, Freedom movement, which embraced more middle-class participation, the tweets contained direct references to the middle class in urban centers as the social sector that benefited from the current system. Within the middle class, also, the tweets had a particular target: writers, journalists, academics, and celebrities who used their platforms to normalize the Republic's violence. The intelligentsia helps the state normalize narratives that describe sociopolitical circumstances and explain relations of power.

> *they butcher every word so ruthlessly / that after each sentence they utter / their teeth and chins are covered in blood / poor words! / poor truth!*

"They," thus, continue to rule in a normalized state of untruth and violence.

"I": Trauma, Despair, and Loneliness

> *suffocation / again / which mass-stranding whale tribe do i belong to? / i haven't caused this mess / i shouldn't crumple on my own / will the tribe die with me?*

The "I" poems represent post-traumatic expressions of loneliness, anxiety, uncertainty, and depression. I discuss these tweets after the "They" section in order to create a flow in the narrative that can help us make sense of the protesters' emotional withdrawal after the Republic's crackdowns, resulting in the detainment, torture, and death of the protesters. The dominant theme is that if the protesters are lucky enough to survive the violence, they find themselves withdrawn in their loneliness and in their tormented self:

> *you are knocking in vain / i have left me / nobody's home!*

When street presence ends, protesters need to resume everyday activities. Nevertheless, the trauma they have experienced will not be easily forgotten. If not killed, injured, or arrested by the police, protesters try to resume their everyday lives, withdrawn into a mental space crowded with the memory of the trauma. Without fellow protesters around them, and having moved back into everyday socialization, protesters find it difficult to function normally in pre-protest social circles. They feel they constantly need to struggle with a sense of loneliness and alienation in their interactions with others:

> *i carry my body around as an everyday obligation / in their company, i put a polite smile on / i pretend that with every step, a part of my flesh is not decaying / that with every breath, a piece of my heart is not rotting / i keep being polite because they are always around / no, you can never be alone in this jungle of loneliness*

In this period of emotional alienation, even one's "body," "smile," and "breath" are no longer part of the self anymore. They are an "obligation." And "politeness" is not a method of connection but a strategy to create distance. The only choice under these circumstances is self-preservation by withdrawing into one's loneliness.

For people who experience crackdowns, this sense of loneliness can become unbearable. Many choose to leave the country as a form of emotional escape. After each wave of protests in Iran, the protesters who have the financial means decide to emigrate—most often unhappily, but as a strategy to preserve their mental well-being:

Sample 10 (Translation: *I will leave this country. If I cannot immigrate legally, I will do it illegally. #immigration*)

Sample 11 (Translation: *It's final. I'm not going to get married and start a family here. I don't want to stay here. I will go anywhere I can. The further, the better. #immigration*)

Sample 12 (Translation: *I wish I could put our house, my bedroom, my parents … put all of these in my suitcase and emigrate. #immigration*)

Statistics also reflect the same reality. Based on a 2020 survey carried out at Tehran's Sharif University, 40% of university students, 53% of university professors, and 45% of health workers who participated in the survey expressed a strong desire to move to another country if possible (Iran Migration Observatory, 2020).

Can taking refuge in one's loneliness or leaving the country heal emotional wounds that protesters endure after each crackdown? The tweets that I collected show that neither self-preservation by withdrawing into individual spaces nor emigration can heal the trauma that the protesters experience. Bedroom quarantines can hardly restore peace of mind because the trauma continues to live in protesters' heads:

> *it feels like my mind will never be tidy / all these flying bits and whirling pieces / my mind is a bankrupt merchant's warehouse*

The chaos, thus, never ends; it just moves from the streets to protesters' minds. Emigration is no relief either. Read the following poem about protesters' disillusionment after immigration:

> *i left my home with a naive plan: leave the ruins behind / alas, the ruins are inside me / wherever I go, I look inside and hurt / i close my eyes: all I see is debris / i open my eyes: all I see is dust*

Farsi Twitter users who succeeded in leaving the country, similar to those who stayed, reported feelings of confused thinking, detachment from reality, helplessness, despair, and mental exhaustion:

> *my head is a suitcase on a baggage claim conveyor belt / turning / turning / turning / the passenger has left it behind*

Post-immigration depression was a major theme on Farsi Twitter. The protesters who left the country would carry the psychological impact of the trauma with them. Also, often, they followed the news about the deteriorating status of the country and new rounds of protests, which triggered the trauma again. Here are a few examples of such tweets:

Sample 13 (Translation: *After two years of struggling with depression, I have decided to emigrate to heal myself and my family. Response to the tweet: Even immigration didn't help with our depression.*)

Sample 14 (Translation: *At this moment, I feel I'm suffering from post-immigration depression, existential depression, and depression as a result of thinking about the situation in Iran.*)

Sample 15 (Translation: *For this obligatory emigration and for my mother's crying over the phone whenever I call her .... For this separation. For this torture.*)

Interestingly, some of the tweets with similar expressions of withdrawal, alienation, and emotional paralysis contain additional themes that connote ideas of resistance. In these tweets, feelings of sadness, loneliness, and fear contribute to the formation of unexpected manifestations of resistance. For instance, in the following poem, see the paradoxical conceptualization of "pain" as a form of "resistance," as if being traumatized is evidence of existence and confirmation of the possibility of resurrection:

> *i'm a crow gazing at january through glass kaleidoscopic eyes / winter has plans, grand and ignoble / i decide that winter cannot freeze me dead / i sit here and watch january's brutal grandeur, as it crystallizes all the life on earth / death is here all around me / the steam rising from my tears warms my head / pain beats*

In some other tweets, a sense of despair is delicately juxtaposed with a desire to be part of a community rather than being presented as the cause of a misanthropic individualism that embraces loneliness as a solution. For instance, the following poem describes the same feeling of loneliness, but not as a result of the individual's preference, rather due to separation from intimate company. The poem is an extended metaphor likening a lonely lover to a wandering "art lover" in search of lost company, with a desire to restore companionship.

> *since you left, i have become an art lover: / i peruse paintings to relocate your color / listen to every note, searching for the waves of your voice / i walk around downtown statues towering above our favorite ice cream booths to savor the remains of your presence*

These two poems, as representatives of tweets that describe both the disturbed circumstances of "I" after the protests and, at the same time, their desire for reconnecting with allies in order to re-create networks of resistance, allow us to make a transition to the next group of poems, where a focus on "I" is replaced with an overt consciousness about the necessity of re-seeking the other, the old companions scattered around and crushed by "They":

> *could i temper the sorrow caused by this separation? / if at least I knew how many cities are between us / what do they call you now? an immigrant? alien?*

"You": Radical Love and Political Romance

The next group of tweets contained romantic lyrical texts that address a partner. I collected these tweets and put them together under the label "You" to imagine how the protesters creep out of their trauma, loneliness, and alienation to reach out to their allies in hopes of reunification and rebuilding communities of resistance. The large size of these tweets in my data pool led me to develop my interpretation of the tweets with the following motif: Protesters at some point have this realization that it is not a state of seclusion that can heal their trauma, but reconnecting with allies and companions:

> *come closer and see the marks of your absences / the burns and bruises / no, nobody can kiss them away / but we might happen to kiss again to remember*

Or in another example:

> *your smell is in my breath; your breath is in my thoughts; my thoughts are in your hair; your hair is the clouds; the clouds are in my head; you are a cloud in my head; you never left; you're always raining in me; and i always smell of the rain in your hair.*

Facing fear with the strength provided by a sense of being part of a community has been a constant discourse in the protests. In protest after protest, people have shouted the chant "Don't fear. We are all together" in the streets and have tweeted it with the hashtag #ما_همه_با_هم_هستیم (#We_are_all_together):

Sample 16 (Translation: #*We_are_all_together*)

Accordingly, in the narrative that I am using to present my discussion of the findings of this project, the "You" poems demonstrate a need for companionship after a period of fear and desperation, a desire to again be in a community that allows reconstructing and redefining the self in relation to others. In this narrative frame, the period of separation ends with expressions of emotional reunification:

> *my immortal blues bleed to a colorful death when your rainbow smile rises above the pathetic battle of daily survival*

And in another example:

> *have you ever seen a singing cloud? / the ones that sob with a heavy, gloomy lump in their hearts? / my girl's hair is made of those clouds, and so are my eyes / all I can see are dark lyrical curves*

One important feature of most of the tweets grouped under the heading "You" is that the romanticism in these tweets, which symbolizes the coming together of the protesters, is by no means a form of lyrical sentimentalism; instead, it is a form of political action that incorporates love as a necessary means of resistance and protest. Interestingly, most of these tweets use metaphorical language that employs elements (images, words, meanings, etc.) that immediately remind us of the people's struggles against an oppressive regime. Read, for instance, the following poem based on a tweet that invokes military and police violence as metaphorical imagery used to describe the beauty of the beloved in the form of poetic irony:

> *the coup d'état of your rose lip rouge / the police dogs of your eyes / and again, you throw me behind your eyelashes' cage bars / where are my human rights?*

Or this poem that paradoxically uses a description of the "bureaucracy" of the state to describe a desire for companionship and intimacy:

> *you and the bureaucracy of your love / every day a new Emotions Report Form / a missing box on the checklist, a meeting, a cancellation, a missing signature / communication issues / and when the submission is complete / your "tomorrow, tomorrow, tomorrow…" / it's getting late / the decision should be made now*

And in the next poem, the beloved is described as a sociopolitical system that fails to deliver justice:

> *i am jealous of your dress / it gets to rest in the aroma of your bosom / self-indulgently / no, there is no justice in the world!*

In these poems, Farsi Twitter users who have experienced or been exposed to the Republic's violence take their trauma with them into their most intimate moments, as if they are chased by a recurring nightmare, and they project their traumatic experiences onto their relationships with the people they love and need most. This process can be described as a psychological defense mechanism, a form of displacement. Displacement is defined as "shifting emotions onto another target considered more acceptable or less threatening" (Furnham, 2012, p. 725). Replacing the beloved with the government makes emotions about the trauma more manageable. When descriptions of the violence that the protesters have endured are juxtaposed with romantic love, it gives their metaphorical reconstruction of the violence in their tweets a tinge of humor and thus helps them revisit the trauma in a less intimidating way. We also know that humor itself is a mature form of psychological defense mechanism (Furnham, 2012).

Next to a strategy of displacement for psychological relief, the poems portray liberatory imagination discovered within intimate companionship as a source of healing and revitalization:

> *lost in your orange imagination / i drink the night with all its seeds, pulp, and bubbles / you imagine a revolution; i bleed on tarmac / you picture a dance; I become a black beauty mark on your rosy cheek / this dance will take two*

The beloved's imagination is a reservoir of demands

long ignored; a chamber of voices long silenced. Repressed desires will soon resurface in an explosion that will cause a radical transformation:

> *you are a pomegranate wrapped tight in your secret swollen truth seeds / inside your sealed existence, invisible cracks are growing / sooner or later, your cheeks will be stained red, bleeding with expression*

Thus, although separated by the Republic's crackdown, the protesters come back together in a radical love for revolutionary resurrection.

In the "You" poems, there are also other motifs that provide more details about the sociopolitical contexts. I end this section with two examples of these sub-motifs. In the following poem, the beloved is a working-class minimum-wage earner. They lack concentration because of their workload, an indication of difficult work conditions:

> *i have a plan / i'll evaporate into an aromatic thought and penetrate your daydreams while you are on your 15-minute lunch break on minimum wage / while exhaustion steals your concentration*

And in the next poem, there is a reference to the current environmental disaster in Iran, again with the paradoxical metaphor of likening "love" to "plastic," as if the persona, in an act of psychological displacement, wished that their love had the longevity of plastic:

> *my love for you is as everlasting as a plastic bag / it'll remain around for thousands of years / it will outlive*

> *your garden's trees and your children's dreams / this sick / plastic / love / … if you had joined me, plastic wouldn't have been invented / trees wouldn't disappear / and children's dreams would come true*

"It": "Things" of the Social Movement

I have called this section the "Things" of the social movement because many of the poems in this section make metaphorical use of objects to describe the characteristics, means, and instruments of the protests. These poems focus on conceptualizations that, in the form of micro-philosophies, reflect the necessity of protest for radical transformation. The "It" poems contain a variety of subjects, including those that echo the previous themes of loneliness, anxiety, and depression, and at the same time a desire for companionship. In these poems, however, objects are placed at the center of the metaphor; for instance, "books" replacing physical human intimacy:

> *in my loneliness, i've read books in all the sex positions you can imagine.*

Or "candles," connoting the absence of loyal friends:

> *the loyalty of a candle / dances when you're joyful / and cries when you are sad*

Among the different subjects appearing in the "It" poems, I highlight a few themes that better connect with the narrative I have been developing. In some of the tweets, protesters deconstruct and redefine seemingly self-explanatory concepts that typically carry positive connotations. Some significant examples are "hope," "God," and "life." In the tweets that I collected, "hope" is described as loaded with the misleading meaning of belief in a better future that will never come. In contrast to its regular meaning, "hope" is an instrument of deception. It is part of a larger design for the state's propaganda to picture a rosy future in the far distance to delay sociopolitical transformation. In the Iranian context, this reconstruction of the meaning of the word "hope" is mainly a reaction to the repeated failures of a political faction referred to as the Reformists. For decades, the Republic has managed public anger through discourses of reform, which promised change but delivered more restrictions and violence. The Reformists' claims for change only prolonged the survival of the oppressive system (Gasiorowski, 2001; Masroori, 2007). Farsi Twitter users advise us that reformist "hope" does not breed much:

> *hope is the opium of the oppressed.*

The replacement of "religion" with "hope" in the well-known quotation "religion is the opium of the people" does not mean that Farsi Twitter is hesitant to address religiosity as a main cause of the Republic's violence. In the pool of tweets collected for this project, there were many examples of characterizations of God that challenged connotations of sacredness, wisdom, care, and power typically associated with the word "God," particularly as these qualities are constantly praised in a theocratic republic. Here are a few examples of the

God poems, curated in the section "He":

> *God, you'd better pray that you're a figment of human's Imagination / otherwise on the Day of Judgment / i'll make you pay for your incompetence*

Or:

> *who knows? God might be another rich snob with lots of stupid ideas*

As these representative poems show, one major theme in the God poems is "incompetence." In these poems, God, or "He," is a metaphor for an incompetent theocracy that is not capable of providing the basic needs of society and has, therefore, prevented people from enjoying a normal life with basic human rights and social freedoms. In this context, more presence of God equals less life.

"Life" is another key discourse on Farsi Twitter. The Republic has failed to maintain normal everyday life by providing basic social freedoms and a reasonably functioning economic system, such as women's right to wear the clothes they choose. A state of misery that the crackdowns on the protests have only deteriorated. This broken administrative system has created a brand of life that edges toward dreadful "surrealism":

> *The surrealism of everyday life's realism: How exciting! How scary!*

This form of life can at best offer a precarious existence:

> *Life is a frothy dream in the broken crest of a stormy ocean wave*

The hashtag زندگی_نرمال# [#normal_life] has for years brought together Iranians' expressions of their horror at everyday manifestations of the Republic's incompetence and has enabled them to list examples of "normal things" that remain unattainable to them. Here are some examples:

Sample 17 (Translation: *Each time I want to drink bootlegged vodka, I look at my loved ones because it might be the last time I see them. #normal_life* [There is a history of people dying in Iran from consuming contaminated illegal spirits.])

Sample 18 (Translation: *#normal_life means you don't need to check your [compulsory] headscarf six hundred times a day to make sure the guy sitting next to you is not "aroused" by your hair.*)

azad @azad14715792 · Dec 31, 2020

#زندگی_نرمال یعنی آزادی با یک زندگی متوسط با توان خرید مایحتاج زندگی خورد و خوراک داشتن خانه کوچک دو اتاق آپارتمانی و تفریحات معمولی که جمهوری اسلامی قادر به برآورده کردن آنها نیست #FinishTheRegime

5 5

Sample 19 (Translation: *#normal_life means freedom and an average life with enough financial means to have food, a small apartment, and some fun, the basics that the Islamic Republic is not able to provide.*)

As these examples show, the hashtag curates multiple everyday objects that represent a normal life violently taken away from the people. A few years after the tweets for this book were selected, the word "life" reappeared as essential component of the slogan "Woman, Life, Freedom" during the 2022 protests. In his *From Hitler to Codreanu: The Ideology of Fascist Leaders*, Martins (2021) explains that in authoritarian states there is often a tension between public and private life that erodes simple everyday freedoms. Martins illustrates this characteristic by sharing the example of the ideas of Oswald Mosley, the founder of the British Union of Fascists (BUF):

> There is also a tension (even if not a real contradiction) between the concepts of 'Public' and 'Private'. Its pertinence is manifest when Mosley talks about how a strong government can limit individual freedoms. … The Authoritarian Corporate State, so he argues, must find a balance between the seemingly contradictory concepts of public and private, creating a Nation where private affairs are permitted (as

> long as they do not run against national interests) but where the State controls the main aspects of public life and the new fascist man is capable of fully committing itself to the public cause. (p. 88)

In such a sociopolitical context, everyday objects—everyday "Things" like ice-cream, vodka, pizza, women's garments, and so on—turn into ideological statements, prompting the state to obsessively target them as political objects that can undermine its authority, depending on how they are used in public spaces.

In response to the Republic's paranoia about "Things," some of the poems portray everyday objects as potential instruments of change. In this group of poems, "Things" can symbolize alternative possibilities. The poetic representation of "Things" in these tweets allows the objects to carry meanings that connote transformation. See, for instance, the use of "rice paddies" in the following poem. The liberty felt in the openness of rice paddies offers protesters a poetic redemption in the face of the claustrophobic depression felt after the protests:

> *our apartment is shrinking / the walls are aggressively closing in on us / these four concrete panels will kill us soon / let's close our eyes and think of rice paddies / let's close our eyes and get our feet wet / with the water around the rice plants of our imagination / sometimes it's only imagination that can liberate*

In another example, we can see how labor tools are

magically used to fix society rather than run the elite's offices, schools, businesses, and military structures. See how in the following poem a cleaner's scrub turns into a magic wand to fundamentally transform the world:

> *i need a colossal scrub to cleanse the world / and loud battle songs to wash out brain dregs and unclog veins*

Interpreting these poems as a continuation of the protesters' desire for social transformation can help us see how they redevelop revolutionary optimism after crackdowns and prepare to initiate a new round of protests. The next section, "We," is meant to represent the final part of this narrative, when the movement's fluctuations bring protesters together in another collective attempt to change the situation.

"We": The Revolutionary Rendezvous

> *i am looking for someone to waste my time with / isn't that a form of activism?*

In my poetic narrative, the cycle of loneliness and depression ends when the protesters once again hear one another, reach out to each other, and come together as "We." The "We" poems describe the protesters' experience of oppression and their resistance in a language tightly and intricately woven with intense lyrical romanticism. In this section, we see an intensification of the portrayal of love as political activism, as well as love as revolution.

> *i saw it in her eyes / her eyes had seen the catastrophe / the choice for me now was either to focus on her eyes / or on the catastrophe*

The "catastrophe" is most visible when recognized in the eyes of the beloved, as if without the love for the other, proper perception of the nature of oppression is not possible because oppression alienates and separates people so that individuals accept current circumstances as "natural." When people get together and share their stories, the common enemy becomes visible. The poem reminds us that "romance" and "resistance" are two sides of the same coin. This conceptualization helps us see the association between "love" and "revolution" more clearly. They share the same nature. Involvement in one prepares us for the other:

> *there are no rules in war and in love / so play hard!*

This revolutionary romance will be identified by oppressive forces, and we will be violently punished for it, but we will survive thanks to our collective imagination:

> *enduring such a deep wet wound gives us an advantage / we don't fall dead in blank horror / we can swim the length of a long death in a numb daze / and imagine colorful futures, floating on bloody shades of dewy red*

Nevertheless, to love in times of violence is not easy. There are moments of self-doubt, withdrawal, and lack of confidence. Within this context, an integral component of romance is reminding the other, and reminding the self through the other's presence, that the price of failure at this romance-revolution is too high. We cannot afford to be afraid because what is at stake is "freedom":

> *no, you aren't afraid of heights / you're afraid of flight, of freedom*

And fear can be overcome by the recognition of the power of the self:

> *the liberator is in the mirror / and the tyrant: the dust on the glass*

The "We" poems, thus, end my poetic narrative by highlighting the political potential of the recognition of one's agency and of one's love for the other.

Whose "Truth"? The Violence of Hegemonic Discourses

In the periods when I was working on this project, Farsi Twitter was a space of intense political exchange, mainly intended to organize protests and communicate information about detained, injured, and murdered protesters. For this project, however, I was interested in tweets posted in post-protest periods that contained emotional reflections and expressions. I hoped poetic engagement with these tweets could help me explore the following questions: What do these tweets tell us about the protesters' emotional status in periods between the crackdowns? What do these emotional reactions reveal about social movements and their dynamics? How can I mobilize poetic inquiry to make these non-trending tweets more visible by framing them as literary texts?

In the process of analyzing the tweets, I translated them from Farsi into English while adding poetic elements to maximize their possible meanings. In a second layer of literary treatment, I framed the poems in a narrative that could connect them in a meaningful flow and, at the same time, reflect a faithful account of the protesters' concerns.

In this narrative, the poems represented in "They" construct an image of the system of oppression, the people who run it, and the people who, willingly or unwillingly, sustain the system. The tweets were clear that the Republic is not run based on a subtle design but with overt violence accompanied by a regime of untruth. The state's use of brute force becomes easier when the public is silent about the system's untruth. Manufacturing and controlling the "truth" are major foundations of systems of oppression. Physical violence and coercive control function when the political system establishes its ownership of the "truth." In a system of overt aggression, this happens less by deception and more by the public display of having the power to control the truth. "The goal of propaganda is not to convince someone that you are right, but to demonstrate that you have authority over the truth itself" (McIntyre, 2018, p. 177). Recently, there has been a lot of attention to the relationship between fascist structures and regimes of untruth, and scholars have asked if we are living in an era of post-truth (Lewandowsky et al., 2017; Levitin, 2017;

Sismondo, 2017). The poems constructed in this inquiry manifest the same concern in the Iranian context: fabrication of the truth, and popularizing it, as a key component of oppression. In this sense, a focus on "truth" is not only an epistemological concern. Instead, it is a recognition of the fact that untruth is violence.

What can these poems tell us about how people react to the system's fabricated "truth"? Most people will keep quiet because they know that the system that has the power to control the truth can launch violence and harm them at will. Sectors of society, however, might willingly remain quiet because, no matter how harsh the conditions, they still benefit from the status quo. Judging by the tweets, in the Iranian context, groups of the middle class perform this informed silence although they may not ideologically represent the system. In Farsi Twitter, members of the middle class are often pictured as echoing the Republic's lies for financial gain.

The middle class has always been at the center of studies of social dynamics, with examples ranging from Marxist and Gramscian treatments of the bourgeoisie to recent scholarship, for instance, about the problems with white middle-class anti-racism (Sullivan, 2014). In the context of the Iranian protests, the anger at the hypocrisy of the middle class has been particularly acute because of the theocratic nature of the Republic and its ironic alliance with the middle class. The Iranian middle class does not think or look like the oppressors; in contrast, they are modern, educated, and liberal. However, as the tweets state, they need the system in place to provide them with their privileges, including financial status and cultural dominance.

The alliance with the middle class allows the oppressors to fabricate discourses that exploit people's vulnerabilities to make them accept the system's "truth." For instance, in the context of this study, the hegemonic discourse utilized to silence the majority has been a national discourse about "security." Wars, conflicts, and political instability in the region have allowed the Islamic Republic to amplify the "security" discourse as a silencing strategy by making people believe that any change in the system will result in the destruction of their lives, as witnessed in other countries in the region. This discourse is often spread publicly with the assistance of middle-class journalists, academics, writers, celebrities, and social media influencers, most of whom are directly or indirectly funded by the Islamic Republic.

"For Gramsci ... the intellectuals who produce and diffuse it [knowledge] are not ornamental butterflies but central ideological agents" (Morrell, 1986, p. 737). The Iranians' negative sentiments about middle-class intellectuals confirm the same understanding of the role of the cultural elite in their own context. Mainstream Iranian intellectuals are not trusted by the public and are often viewed as a cause of the problems rather than as people willing or capable of offering solutions. Moreover, since it is the educated members of the middle class who have the means of learning European languages, traveling abroad, studying in Western universities, and communicating with non-Farsi media, the people consider them as instrumental in disseminating the Islamic Republic's untruth internationally.

The poems in the section "I" were arranged to represent the protesters' emotions in the period after the protests were crushed. When the protesters are scattered and forced back to their homes, they withdraw into loneliness and struggle with despair and depression. "Much like the quest for everyday well-being, protest can be mentally, physically, and existentially agonizing to both affected participants, and onlooking others" (Rawlins, 2021, p. 3). There are tweets in post-protest Farsi Twitter that report feelings of anxiety, disillusionment, hopelessness, and indecision. These feelings are experienced individually and in isolation, far from like-minded companions.

Farsi Twitter users frequently shared posts about emigration as an option in response to hopelessness about the possibility of any meaningful change. There are no reliable statistics about the size of the Iranian diaspora, but there are estimates that more than 5 million people might have left the country since the establishment of the Islamic Republic in 1979. Each protest has led to a peak in emigration numbers. Protesters' well-being is not only threatened at home as a result of traumatic experiences, but there has also been research warning about mental health issues among Iranians who have left the country (Jafari et al., 2010; Nahidi, S., Blignault et al., 2018). There are reports of depression and homesickness in the diaspora, triggered by anxiety about the developments in Iran. Hence, emigration does not appear to be a reliable remedy for the psychological pressure.

Nevertheless, in the "I" poems, there are still some expressions of resistance: "*death is all there is around me / ...i cry / the steam rising from my tears warms my head / pain beats.*" These tweets recognize the power of the oppressors but refuse to accept defeat as the final outcome because desperation can also lead to more resistance. In creating a flow for the narrative that ordered the poems, I ended the "I" section with tweets that carried elements of resistance as a transition to the "You" poems, which narrate a revival of interest in reaching out to ex-companions after a period of isolation.

The poems in the "You" section are based on tweets that express a need for companionship. Companionship, through a revolutionary lens, has a double function. Emotionally, it is a remedy for feelings of post-protest alienation and loneliness. Politically, it is the essential component of the social movement as it revives people's collective power. As a result, stating a need for rebuilding relationships in these poems is characterized by an intense political romanticism which resembles a form of *radical love.* The term "radical love" has long been used to mean extending love, care, and compassion to others and, at the same time, engaging in collective action to change sociopolitical circumstances that separate, demean, and marginalize humans (Freire, 2000, 2007; Gómez, 2015; hooks, 2000; Kincheloe, 2008). Love in this sense is not only a romantic expression, but a political act. "Radical love is a love that bears witness to, with, and for others toward liberation without an expectation of return. It is a love that first and foremost does justice" (Robinson-Morris, 2019, p. 37).

In the "You" section, radical love is expressed through a lyricism that juxtaposes expressions of love with images of the means of oppression. The metaphors that form the lyrical foundation of these poems are constructed through imagery that invokes the constant violence perpetrated by the State, such as "police dogs" and "prison bars." These metaphors are harsh conceits that use this imagery to depict complex forms of politicized love and the experiences of traumatized lovers.

The same kind of political metaphorization is also used in the "It" poems. A similar form of metaphorical radicalism is mobilized to explain concepts, philosophies, and instruments of the protests. Through a process of re-signification, Farsi Twitter users redefined concepts with positive connotations, such as "hope," to explain their movement. They tell us "hope" can be destructive if it delays radical action. They defamiliarize everyday objects such as clothes, fruit, and beverages to display the grotesque lack of liberty that the people are struggling with.

The "We" poems conclude the narrative by bringing "You" and "I" together for a resurrection of protests. After a period of battle fatigue, the declined energy of the movement is restored by this reunification. The theme of radical romanticism and transformative love continues to tinge some of the poems in "We": "*there are no rules in war and in love / so play hard*!" The poignant aspect of this romance is the nightmarish presence of the oppressors' violence even in the lovers' most intimate moments. "*i saw it in her eyes / her eyes had seen the catastrophe / the choice for me now was either to focus on her eyes / or on the catastrophe*".

Despite the continuity of this traumatic brutality in the "We" section, the poems offer solutions toward a radical social transformation. One example is the recognition of the power of the self: "*the liberator is in the mirror / and the tyrant: the dust on the glass.*" Another is prioritizing a demand for "liberty," a concept forgotten because it has long been kept away from the people. "*no, you aren't afraid of heights / you're afraid of flight, of freedom*". Another key strategy is mobilizing the power of collective imagination: "*we don't fall dead in blank horror / we can swim the length of a long death in a numb daze / and imagine colorful futures.*" A suggestion for imagining future possibilities is significant because we know that "imagination helps to constitute communities as political entities" (Moody-Adams, 2022, p. 119). The coming together of "I" and "You" as "We" creates the possibility of collectively imagining alternative futures.

With an emphasis on the emotional world of protesters and the witnesses of the protests, this project is a contribution to new trends in theories of social movements that, as Jasper (2010) argues, "offer a cultural and emotional theory of action" (p. 965). "Inevitably, the intellectual pendulum has swung away from the great structural and historical paradigms and back toward creativity and agency, culture and meaning, emotion and morality" (Jasper, 2010, p. 970). This pendulum swing might not be complete without methodological approaches that can better capture the depth, complexity, and intensity of human feelings. This project, thus, has made use of poetic language to make better sense of the meanings involved in the emotional lives of the Iranians who have been participating in the protests.

Final Remarks: Poetic Inquiry and Pax Technica

I started this project as a response to the silence of the Western media about the massacre of 1,500 protesters in the uprising of November 2019. During the protests, Farsi Twitter became energetically active to spread the word, but the news never became viral in the West. It is certainly relevant to ask what social media posts trend and what posts don't, and how the visibility or invisibility of citizens who are in the midst of protests can impact the life of a social movement.

It is rather paradoxical to think about the invisibility of public online posts because the gift of digital instant posting makes all online texts available to the public. Nevertheless, the attention that online posts receive is regulated by the same technology that provides the online platforms for unfiltered expression. Fabricated trends, algorithms, bots, and cyber armies can significantly impact online discourse creation and mobilization. Howard (2015) argues that, despite earlier promises of free and liberatory circulation of information via the Internet, we are living in an age of *Pax Technica* in which high-tech industries, governments, security apparatuses, and even civil society actors have aligned their visions closely. In this period, the said parties have a peaceful collaboration to create political stability and to preserve the status quo. Not surprisingly, the status quo happens to favor a small economic elite and, at the same time, widens the socioeconomic gap between the elite and the rest of the people. In this scene, the Internet is used to control the information rather than freely circulate it. In the age of Pax Technica, connectivity of ideas is replaced by connective security, the Internet is used to isolate radical ideas, and technological control maintains the sociopolitical structure of states. The same process also protects failed states, such as the Islamic Republic, as long as they don't seriously threaten the global order and international markets.

Through an economic lens, this Pax Technica, protected and promoted by a small elite, has been described and discussed as an emerging era of techno-feudalism (Langman, 1998; Waters, 2020):

> This new political economy can be summarily defined as a system dominated by the ubiquitous presence of technology for social control (mass surveillance, automation of production, artificial intelligence, the Internet of Things) by the rentiers and oligarchs who own the crucial platform networks into which we are all subsumed. (Waters, 2020, p. 408).

It is, thus, ironic that the Internet, believed to be a free highway of information, has turned into an instrument of control in a new form of feudalism.

I previously explained that poetic inquiry helped me explore the meanings of protesters' emotional expressions thanks to the linguistic complexity offered by poetry. If the Internet, in the current Pax Technica, controls and limits the visibility of information about injustices rather than promotes it, another significance of this project is its potential to highlight texts in a non-English language buried under the algorithms of Pax Technica. Poetic representation of these non-trending tweets might preserve the voice of witnesses to an important period in Iranian history. Poetry as a traditional genre has stood the test of time by preserving crucial human experiences and discourses for us. It just seems reasonable to trust the genre to protect the less heard voices of this movement.

Author bio:

Dr. Amir Kalan is an Assistant Professor in the Department of Integrated Studies in Education at McGill University. His research aims to create a sociology of writing that provides insights into the cultural, political, and power-relational dimensions of linguistic and textual practices. He is particularly interested in organic writing practices that occur beyond the current narrow institutional categorizations of writing styles, genres, and rhetorical norms. He is the author of *Who's Afraid of Multilingual Education?* (2016) and *Sociocultural and Power-Relational Dimensions of Multilingual Writing* (2021), and a co-editor of *Critical Action Research Challenging Neoliberal Language and Literacies Education* (2022).

This book is part of Dr. Kalan's broader "Writing in Times of Crisis" research project. "Writing in Times of Crisis" explores writers' experiences during periods of calamity, instability, and uncertainty. The project features multiple studies of communities and individuals engaging with writing and publishing in times of trauma and tragedy. Examples include: teaching and learning writing during pandemics (Kalan, 2021a); immigrants' and refugees' engagement with writing in additional languages (Kalan, 2021b, 2021c); the rhetoric of protest (Kalan, 2021d); and transnational students' experiences with writing across borders and cultures (Kalan, 2022, 2024).

References

Allen, A. A., & Simon, R. (2021). Unsettling a canonical text through erasure poetry. *English Journal, 110*(5), 43-50.

Azadi, P., & Mesgaran, M. B. (2021). *The clash of ideologies on Persian Twitter* (Working Paper No. 10). Stanford Iran 2040 Project, Stanford University.

Bakhtin, M. M. (1981). *The dialogic imagination: Four essays* (M. Holquist, Ed.; C. Emerson & M. Holquist, Trans.). University of Texas Press.

Bauman, R., & Briggs, C. L. (1990). Poetics and performance as critical perspectives on language and social life. *Annual Review of Anthropology, 19*, 59-88.

Brock, A. (2012). From the Blackhand side: Twitter as a cultural conversation. *Journal of Broadcasting & Electronic Media, 56*(4), 529-549.

Burns, A. & Eltham, B. (2009). Twitter free Iran: An evaluation of Twitter's role in public diplomacy and information operations in Iran's 2009 Election Crisis. In Papandrea, F. and Armstrong, M. (Eds.) Record of the communications policy & research forum 2009. Network Insight Pty Ltd. Available at https://vuir.vu.edu.au/15230/1/CPRF09BurnsEltham.pdf

Butler-Kisber, L. (2010). Poetic inquiry. In L. Butler-Kisber (Ed.), *Qualitative inquiry: Thematic, narrative and arts-informed perspectives* (pp. 82-120). Los Angeles, CA: Sage.

Carlson, B., & Berglund, J. (Eds.). (2021). *Indigenous peoples rise up: The global ascendency of social media activism.* Rutgers University Press.

Carlson, B., & Frazer, R. (2021). Anger, hope, and love. In B. Carlson & J. Berglund (Eds.), *Indigenous peoples rise up: The global ascendency of social media activism* (pp. 48-64). Rutgers University Press.

Chan, Z. C. Y. (2003). Poetry writing: A therapeutic

means for a social work doctoral student in the process of study. *Journal of Poetry Therapy, 16*, 5-17.

Dill, L. J., Vearey, J., Oliveira, E., & Castillo, G. M. (2016). "Son of the Soil… Daughters of the Land": poetry writing as a strategy of citizen-making for lesbian, gay, and bisexual migrants and asylum seekers in Johannesburg. *Agenda, 30*(1), 85-95.

Downing, J. D. H. (2014). Social Movement media in the process of constructive social change. In K. G. Wilkins, T. Tufte, & R. Obregon (Eds.), *The Handbook of development communication and social change* (pp. 331–350). John Wiley and Sons.

Effing, R., Hillegersberg, J. V., & Huibers, T. (2011). Social media and political participation: are Facebook, Twitter and YouTube democratizing our political systems? In *International conference on electronic participation* (pp. 25-35). Springer, Berlin, Heidelberg.

Faulkner, S. L. (2017). Poetic inquiry: Poetry as/in/for social research. In P. Leavy (Ed.), *The handbook of arts-based research* (pp. 208-230). New York, NY: Guilford Press.

Freire, P. (2000). *Pedagogy of the oppressed.* New York, NY: Continuum. (Original work published 1970)

Freire, P. (2007). *Education for critical consciousness.* New York, NY: Continuum. (Original work published 1974)

Furman, R. (2004). Using poetry and narrative as qualitative data: Exploring a father's cancer through poetry. *Families, Systems, & Health, 22*(2), 1-9.

Furnham, A. (2012). Lay understandings of defence mechanisms: The role of personality traits and gender. *Psychology, Health & Medicine, 17*(6), 723-734.

Galvin, K., & Prendergast, M. (Eds.). (2012). Special issue: Poetic inquiry. *Creative Approaches to Research, 5*(2), 1-180.

Gasiorowski, M. J. (2001). Iran under Khatami: Deadlock or change? *Global Dialogue, 3*(2), 9-18.

Gil de Zúñiga, H., Huber, B., & Strauß, N. (2018). Social media and democracy. *El Profesional de la Información (EPI), 27*(6), 1172–1180.

Gómez, J. (2015). *Radical love: A revolution for the 21st century.* New York, NY: Peter Lang.

Goodwin, J., Jasper, J. M., & Polletta, F. (Eds.). (2001). *Passionate politics: Emotions and social movements.* University of Chicago Press.

Grossman, L. (2009). Iran protests: Twitter, the medium of the movement. *Time Magazine* [Online]. Available at: http://www.time.com/time/world/article/0?8599,1905125,00.html (25 May 2010).

Halpern, D., Valenzuela, S., & Katz, J. E. (2017). We face, I tweet: How different social media influence political participation through collective and internal efficacy. *Journal of Computer-Mediated Communication, 22*(6), 320-336.

Hashemi, L., Wilson, S., & Sanhueza, C. (2022). Five hundred days of Farsi Twitter: An overview of what Farsi Twitter looks like, what we know about it, and why it matters. *Journal of Quantitative Description: Digital Media*, 2, 1–29.

hooks, b. (2000). *All about love: New visions.* New York: Harper Perennial.

Howard, P. N. (2015). *Pax Technica: How the Internet of things may set us free or lock us up.* Yale University Press.

Iran Migration Observatory (2020). Migration statistics retrieved from https://imobs.ir/

Jafari, S., Baharlou, S., & Mathias, R. (2010). Knowledge of determinants of mental health among Iranian immigrants of BC, Canada: "A qualitative study." *Journal of Immigrant and Minority Health, 12*(1), 100-106.

Jasper, J. M. (2010). Social movement theory today: Toward a theory of action? *Sociology Compass, 4*(11), 965-976.

Kalan, A. (2021a). COVID-19, an opportunity to deindustrialize writing education. In I. Fayed, & J. Cummings (Eds.), *Teaching in the post COVID-19 era: World education dilemmas, teaching innovations and solutions in the age of crisis* (pp. 511-519). Springer.

Kalan, A. (2021b). Writing in times of crisis: A theoretical model for understanding genre formation. In E. B. Hancı-Azizoğlu, & M. Alawdat (Eds.), *Rhetoric and sociolinguistics in times of global crisis* (pp. 214-234). IGI Global.

Kalan, A. (2021c). *Sociocultural and power-relational dimensions of multilingual writing: Recommendations for deindustrializing writing education.* Bristol, UK: Multilingual Matters.

Kalan, A. (2021d). A rhetoric of protest [Poem]. The College English Association Mid-Atlantic Review, 29, 78-79.

Kalan, A. (2022). Negotiating writing identities across languages: Translanguaging as enrichment of semiotic trajectories. *TESL Canada Journal, 38*(2), 63-87.

Kalan, A. (2024). "Our culture is a product of active word": A poetic inquiry into immigrants' experiences with writing in a host language. *Art/Research International: A Transdisciplinary Journal, 9*(1), 201–235.

Keller, J., Mendes, K., & Ringrose, J. (2018). Speaking 'unspeakable things': Documenting digital feminist responses to rape culture. *Journal of Gender Studies, 27*(1), 22-36.

Kermani, H., & Adham, M. (2021). Mapping Persian Twitter: Networks and mechanism of political communication in Iranian 2017 presidential election. *Big Data & Society, 8*(1), 1–16.

Kincheloe, J. L. (Ed.). (2008). *Knowledge and critical pedagogy: An introduction.* Dordrecht: Springer Netherlands.

Lane, D. S., Lee, S. S., Liang, F., Kim, D. H., Shen, L., Weeks, B. E., & Kwak, N. (2019). Social media expression and the political self. *Journal of Communication, 69*(1), 49-72.

Langman, L. (1998). Bakhtin the future: Techno-capital and cyber-feudalism. In D. Kalekin-Fishman (Ed.), *Designs for alienation: Exploring diverse realities* (pp. 341-366). SoPhi University of Jyväskylä.

Losh, E. (2014). Hashtag feminism and Twitter activism in India. *Social Epistemology Review and Reply Collective, 3*(3), 11-22.

Namnyak, M., Tufton, N., Szekely, R., Toal, M., Worboys, S., & Sampson, E. L. (2008). 'Stockholm syndrome': Psychiatric diagnosis or urban myth? *Acta Psychiatrica Scandinavica, 117*(1), 4-11.

Lewandowsky, S., Ecker, U. K., & Cook, J. (2017). Beyond misinformation: Understanding and coping with the "post-truth" era. *Journal of Applied Research in Memory and Cognition, 6*(4), 353-369.

Levitin, D. J. (2017). *Weaponized lies: How to think critically in the post-truth era.* Penguin.

McIntyre, L. (2018). *Post-truth.* MIT Press.

Martins, C. M. (2021). *From Hitler to Codreanu: The ideology of fascist leaders.* Routledge.

Masroori, C. (2007). The conceptual obstacles to political reform in Iran. *The Review of Politics, 69*(2), 171-191.

Metallic, J. E. (2017). *Nta'tugwaqannminen our stories: Language stories and experiences of young adult Mi'gmaq learners* (Unpublished doctoral dissertation). McGill University, Montreal, QC.

Meyer, E. J. (2008). "Who We Are Matters": Exploring teacher identities through found poetry. *LEARNing Landscapes, 2*(1), 195-210.

Mills, C. W. (1959). *The Sociological Imagination.* New York: Oxford University Press.

Moody-Adams, M. M. (2022). *Making space for justice:*

Social movements, collective imagination, and political hope. Columbia University Press.
Morrell, J. (1986). Brains of Britain. *Social Studies of Science, 16*(4), 735-745.
Morozov, E. (2009). Iran: Downside to the "Twitter revolution". *Dissent, 56*(4), 10-14.
Mukerji, C. (2018). It goes without saying: Imagination, inarticulacy, and materiality in political culture. In L. Grindstaff, M. M. Lo, & J. R. Hall (Eds.), *Routledge handbook of cultural sociology* (pp. 113-121). Routledge.
Nahidi, S., Blignault, I., Hayen, A., & Razee, H. (2018). Psychological distress in Iranian international students at an Australian university. *Journal of Immigrant and Minority Health, 20*(3), 651-657.
Nau, C., Zhang, J., Quan-Haase, A., & Mendes, K. (2022). Vernacular practices in digital feminist activism on Twitter: deconstructing affect and emotion in the #MeToo movement. *Feminist Media Studies*, 1-17.
Papacharissi, Z. (2002). The virtual sphere: The internet as a public sphere. *New Media & Society, 4*(1), 9-27.
Papacharissi, Z. (2010). *A networked self: Identity, community, and culture on social network sites*. Routledge.
Papacharissi, Z. (2015). *Affective publics: Sentiment, technology, and politics*. Oxford University Press.
Park, C. S. (2013). Political carnivalism and an emerging public space: Examination of a new participatory culture on Twitter. *International Journal of Electronic Governance, 6*(4), 302-318.
Phipps, A., Ringrose, J., Renold, E., & Jackson, C. (2018). Rape culture, lad culture and everyday sexism: Researching, conceptualizing and politicizing new mediations of gender and sexual violence. *Journal of Gender Studies, 27*(1), 1-8.
Pingree, R. J. (2007). How messages affect their senders: A more general model of message effects and implications for deliberation. *Communication Theory*,

17(4), 439-461.

Prendergast, M. (2009). Introduction: The phenomena of poetry in research. In M. Prendergast, C. Leggo, and P. Sameshima (Eds.), *Poetic inquiry: Vibrant voices in the social sciences* (pp. xix–xlii). Rotterdam: Sense.

Prendergast, C. Leggo, & P. Sameshima, P. (Eds.). (2009). *Poetic inquiry: Vibrant voices in the social sciences.* Boston: Sense Publishers.

Rawlins, L. S. (2021). "It was something that is a necessity": Stories of collective protest, vulnerability, and well-being. *Health Communication*, 1-3.

Robinson-Morris, D. W. (2019). Radical love, (r)evolutionary becoming: Creating an ethic of love in the realm of education through Buddhism and Ubuntu. *The Urban Review, 51*(1), 26-45.

Rodríguez, I. S. (2019). The technopolitical frameworks of contemporary social movements. In C. F. Fominaya, & R. Feenstra (Eds.), *Routledge Handbook of Contemporary European Social Movements: Protest in Turbulent Times* (pp. 313- 325). Routledge.

Saldaña, M., McGregor, S. C., & Gil de Zúñiga, H. (2015). Social media as a public space for politics: Cross-national comparison of news consumption and participatory behaviors in the United States and the United Kingdom. *International Journal of Communication, 9*(1), 3304-3326.

Siapera, E., Boudourides, M., Lenis, S., & Suiter, J. (2018). Refugees and network publics on Twitter: Networked framing, affect, and capture. *Social Media + Society, 4*(1), 1-21.

Sismondo, S. (2017). Post-truth? *Social Studies of Science, 47*(1), 3-6.

Smithka, P. (2022). The Lies of the Land: Post-truth, the Erosion of Democracy, and the Challenge for Positive Peace. In S. Lal (Ed.), *Peaceful approaches for a more peaceful world* (pp. 170-195). Brill.

Shahi, A., & Abdoh-Tabrizi, E. (2020). Iran's 2019–2020

demonstrations: The changing dynamics of political protests in Iran. *Asian Affairs, 51*(1), 1-41.

Shayesteh, F., & Seo, H. (2022). Competing frames on social media: Analysis of English and Farsi tweets on Iran plane crash. *The Journal of International Communication, 28*(1), 47-69.

Sullivan, S. (2014). *Good white people: The problem with middle-class white anti-racism*. SUNY Press.

Thomas, S., Cole, A. L., & Stewart, S. (2012). *The art of poetic inquiry*. Big Tancook Island, Nova Scotia, Canada: Backalong.

Tsugawa, S., Kikuchi, Y., Kishino, F., Nakajima, K., Itoh, Y., & Ohsaki, H. (2015, April). Recognizing depression from twitter activity. In *Proceedings of the 33rd annual ACM conference on human factors in computing systems* (pp. 3187-3196).

Wang, J., & Wei, L. (2020). Fear and hope, bitter and sweet: Emotion sharing of cancer community on twitter. *Social Media + Society, 6*(1), 1-12.

Waters, A. (2020). Will neoliberal capitalism survive the coronavirus crash or is this the beginning of techno-feudalism? *Journal of Australian Political Economy, 86*, 406-431.

Williams, S. (2015). Digital defense: Black feminists resist violence with hashtag activism. *Feminist Media Studies, 15*(2), 341-344.

Wonneberger, A., Hellsten, I. R., & Jacobs, S. H. (2021). Hashtag activism and the configuration of counterpublics: Dutch animal welfare debates on Twitter. *Information, Communication & Society, 24*(12), 1694-1711.

Xue, J., Chen, J., Hu, R., Chen, C., Zheng, C., Su, Y., & Zhu, T. (2020). Twitter discussions and emotions about the COVID-19 pandemic: Machine learning approach. *Journal of Medical Internet Research, 22*(11), 1-14.

Asemana Books

Devoted to Publishing Diasporic, Underrepresented and Progressive Literature on the Middle East.

Email: Asemanabooks@gmail.com
Webpage: asemanabooks.ca

Scholarly and Academic Research

- *Iranian Solar Calendar and Endurance of Nowruz in Persian Time Culture* – Abbas Amanat – 2025
- *Theatre in Travel*– Duman Riyazi– 2025
- *Tanglusha of a Thousand Images: Essays on Culture and Literature* – Reza Farokhfal – 2024
- *Language, People, and Society: Iranian Minority Languages and Literary Traditions* – Edited by Amir Kalan, Mahdi Ganjavi, Anisa Jafari, Lale Javanshir – 2024
- *Music on the Borderland: Remembering and Chronicling the 1979 Revolution's Shadow on Iranian Music* – Keyan Emami – 2024
- *Implications of Class Analysis in Capitalist Imperialism* – Mohammad Hajinia and Shahrzad Mojab – 2024
- *Dark Night and Phoenixes of the Ashes: Nima Yushij's Poetry from 1932–1942* – Ramin Ahmadi – 2024
- *Whispers of Oasis: Likoo's Poetic Mirage* – Mahdi Ganjavi, Amin Fatemi, Mansour Alimoradi – 2024
- *Hafez and Irony* – Reza Farokhfal – 2024
- *Kurdish Women at the Core of the Historical Contradictions on Feminism and Nationalism* – Shahrzad Mojab – 2023

- *The Peasant Uprising of Mukriyan 1952–1953: Consulate Documents, Diplomatic Correspondence, and the Press Coverage* – Amir Hassanpour – 2022

Memoirs

- *Adventures of Pen and Lens*– Reza Allamehzadeh – 2026
- *Colour and Mystery* Irene Monique Salehi – 2025

Critical Edition

- *The Basil that Enlightens the Garden*– Mirza Agha Khan Kermani, edited by M. Rezaei Tazik – 2025
- *The Art of Speaking and Writing* – Mirza Agha Khan Kermani, edited by M. Rezaei Tazik – 2025
- *Creation and Legislation* – Mirza Agha Khan Kermani, edited by M. Rezaei Tazik – 2025
- *The History of Changes in Iran* – Mirza Agha Khan Kermani, edited by M. Rezaei Tazik – 2024
- *Rostam in the Twenty-Second Century* – Abdulhussain San'atizadeh Kermani, edited by Mahdi Ganjavi and M. Mansouri – 2017

Poetry

- *The World Stares at Me. And I at Heart* – Bijan Safdari – 2026
- *My dreams breathe in broken fragments*– Hadi Ebrahimi Roudbaraki - 2026
- *Prism of Wounded Light* – Amin Haddadi, Translated by Dariush Shahinrad - 2025.

- *Shape of Extinction* – Poetry of Bijan Jalali, Translated by Adeeba Shahid Talukder and Aria Fani - 2025
- *One Hundred Nights of Yearning* – Mansour Noorbakhsh – 2025
- *Songs of Barbad* – Amir Hakimi – 2024
- *With My Shadows, I Created Myself* – Hadi Ebrahimi Roudbaraki - 2024
- *Citizens of September* – Saeid Rezadoust - 2024
- *Wonder of Memory* – Amir Hakimi – 2023
- *Galaxy Has No Memory of the Sunset* – Mahdi Ganjavi – 2023
- *Strangers Who Live in Me* – Mahdi Ganjavi – 2021
- *Exiled to the Rocky* – Ali Fatolahi – 2018

Fiction & Plays

- *The Qualities of Children That We Thought Were Stronger Than Bombs*, a novel by Siamak Vossoughi, 2026
- *Our decline*, a novel by Peyman Yarian, 2026
- *The Blue Side of the Sky*, a novel by Javad Alavi, 2026
- *Badri*, a novel by Behrooz Badakhshan, 2025
- *My Husband, My Feather Pillow*, a novel by Fatemeh Zarei, 2025
- *Destined to Lead?* - a novel by Hushang Dowlatabadi, translated by Hadi Dowlatabadi, 2025
- *56 Degrees*, a novel by Hossein Noushazar, 2025
- From The Northwest, short stories by Amirhossein Bakhtiari, 2025
- *An Iranian Odyssey* - a novel by Rana Soleimani, translated by Fereidon Rashidi, 2025
- *Family Secret Memories* - novel by Mohammad Qassemzadeh, translated by Mahshad Abdoli, 2025

- *Stories from Tehran* - short stories by Fereshteh Molavi, 2025.
- *Escape from the Girl's Complex* - Mahbobe Mousavi – 2025
- *Yousef, Joseph, Guiseppe* – Ali Foumani - 2025
- *An Iranian Odyssey* – Rana Soleimani – 2025
- *Lead to Evil* – Javad Alavi – 2025
- *We Are Drunk and Broken, and No One Is Witnessing Us* – Mahdi Ganjavi – 2025
- *Someone Had Died in Front of Our House* – Akbar Falahzadeh – 2024
- *Zinat* – Vahid Zarrabi Nasab – 2024
- *Siberian Crane* – Ali Foumani - 2024
- *Elephants Reached the Plain* – Kaveh Oveisi - 2024
- *Textual Mosaic* – Marzieh Sotoudeh – 2024
- *Expectations of a Dream* – Mahdi Ganjavi – 2020

Asemana Books is devoted to publishing diasporic, underrepresented, and progressive literature on the Middle East.

asemanabooks.ca

ASEMANA
BOOKS

www.ingramcontent.com/pod-product-compliance
Lightning Source LLC
LaVergne TN
LVHW091138080826
845145LV00008B/2196